How to Do Plays with Children

Entire contents of compiled version copyright ©1994
by EVAN-MOOR CORP.
18 Lower Ragsdale Drive, Monterey, CA 93940-5746

Authors: Jo Ellen Moore, Ginny Hall,
Leslie Tryon, Betsy Franco
Illustrators: Joy Evans, Leslie Tryon
Editor: Jo Ellen Moore
Cover Design: Cheryl Kashata,
Gary L. Shipman
Production Assistant: Michelle Tapola

Original editions:
The Shoemaker and the Elves, © 1986 by Evan-Moor Corp.
The Magic Pasta Pot, © 1986 by Evan-Moor Corp.
Things Could Always Be Worse, © 1986 by Evan-Moor Corp.
Spring Starts Here!, © 1987 by Evan-Moor Corp.
A Flea On Santa's Tree?, © 1987 by Evan-Moor Corp.
Goldilocks and the Three Bears, © 1987 by Evan-Moor Corp.
The Little Red Hen, © 1987 by Evan-Moor Corp.
Mother Goose's Goose Is Loose, © 1987 by Evan-Moor Corp.
Headbands for Quick and Easy Play Activities, © 1986 by
Evan-Moor Corp.

"Do you remember when I was a star?"

As teachers we sometimes wonder what long-term impact, if any, we have on our students. One day in the supermarket I was approached by a young woman carrying a baby. After answering her first question ("Didn't you used to be Miss Moore?") in the affirmative, she asked, "Do you remember when I was a star?" She went on to recall dancing on stage in a play in the second grade. I am sure she learned many things that school year. I know we read books, solved math problems, did science experiments, painted pictures, sang songs...however, for that second grade child, performing on stage for an audience was the highlight to be remembered forever.

Performing, both impromptu "plays" or structured plays, provides learnings and satisfactions that are provided by no other experience. Children are learning cooperation, sharing responsibility, and solving problems. Self-esteem is increased. They practice academic skills from subjects across the curriculum using many learning modalities. In addition, performing a play provides many opportunities for school-home connections.

This book contains directions on classroom dramatic play and how to present a formal play for an audience. Various types of plays are also included. Recommendations are given for how to put together your own performances when you cannot find an appropriate play on the topic you need.

Part 1	Getting Ready
Part 2	Play Activities
Part 3	Rhyming Plays
Part 4	Folk Tales
Part 5	Reader's Theater

Use these plays:
- as they are written
- as choral verse
- as reading assignments
- as the basis for student rewrites (to fit another time/area/culture)
- as a model for writing original plays

More Than Just a Play

Use the avenue of dramatic play/performances to create an enriching experience providing both personal and academic rewards.

Self-esteem
• Children experience the successful completion of a project.
• Shy children can build confidence performing within the safety of a group.
• Children have the opportunity to use a variety of talents and skills.
• They can be the center of attention in a positive way.

Sharing
• Children share time and energy in getting the play ready to present.
• They share by performing the play for others - parents, other classes, nursery homes, community groups, etc.

Cooperation and Responsibility
• Children experience putting the needs of the group ahead of their own special interests.
• They have the opportunity to help one another as they prepare for the play.
• They experience being attentive, on time, and prepared.
• They practice working together in both large and small groups.

Problem-Solving
• Children practice problem-solving as they:
>   -determine who will have what part in the play.
>   -decide on costumes, props, and sets.
>   -decide when and where to go for help if it is needed.
• They have the opportunity to solve problems as they determine how costumes, props, and sets will be constructed.

Practice Academic Skills
• Children have the opportunity to practice reading, research, math, art, movement, and music skills.
• They experience applying skills learned elsewhere.

School-Home Connection
• Parents have the opportunity to become involved with the school as they:
>   -help children practice lines.
>   -assist with the making of costumes.
>   -help construct sets.
• Parents show support of their children's education by attending the performance.

 How to Do Plays with Children

"It's too much work." "It takes too much time." "I don't know what to do." Do you recognize yourself in any of these complaints/excuses? In the introduction, you have been given a rationale for spending time and energy on a performance. The rewards in both academic and behavioral terms are great enough to justify the time involved. The tips and techniques in this chapter will help with the "what to do."

Rule 1: Keep it Simple!
First of all, remember that not every play you do needs to be a major production. Do frequent short plays for yourselves or the class next door for fun and practice. Begin simply. Maybe your first performances will be Reader's Theater or the recitation of a selection of poems. Leave the full-fledged, "off-Broadway" productions until you and your students have more experience.

Rule 2: Perfection Isn't the Goal!
Always keep this in mind. I have seen many groups become miserable because an impossible level of perfection was being expected. You want it to be well-done, but not at a loss of the element of joy in the experience.

Rule 3: Ask for Help!
You don't have to do it all yourself. I am going to repeat that for all you Type A teachers out there. You don't have to do it all yourself! Involve parents and other volunteers. Draw on the talents of others in your school and community. You may be surprised at what turns up.

There is a point in preparing for a performance before everything begins to come together, where you may begin to doubt your sanity at starting the whole process. Take a deep breath and look at what is going on. Are you trying to do too much? Are you aiming for a level of perfection beyond the ability of yourself and your class? Are you trying to do everything yourself? If the answer to any of these is yes, make changes right now. If the answer to all of the questions is no, then relax and keep on with practice and preparations, and soon it will all begin to come together.

Dramatic Play Across the Curriculum

Dramatic experiences should not be limited to the presentation of a set play by the class once a year at a school-wide assembly. For children of the television-video generation, "chants," "raps," or "hip-hop" can be the dramatic format of choice for enriching the curriculum, motivating students and evaluating learning.

Reading/Language Arts
Have children think about the characters in the stories they read to themselves or in reading class. Have them practice reading with emotion and in voices that are appropriate to the age and behavior of the character.

Act out the parts of speech both in action and word. Present impromptu plays by acting out stories being read from a reading text or literature book. Begin with short stories or just do a scene from a story. Children plan their own dialogue, and sets consist of whatever you have on hand in class. These may be presented to a small group in class or to the class as a whole.

Math
Act out math problems as a part of solving problems in math class. Not only will your students gain experience in performing for the group, they will improve their visualization skills and ability to figure out the solutions to problems.

Use math skills in creating props, costumes and settings for a formal play presentation.

Science
Have children act out elements of change occurring in nature such as the stages in the growth of an animal or plant or what happens to water as it moves from steam, to liquid, to a solid and back again.

Social Sciences

Again do impromptu presentations of material you read to students or they read themselves. Cultural and holiday celebration, famous speeches, and specific events from history lend themselves to this type of practice presentation. You may find that some of these are so successful they lead to a performance for an audience.

One of the most effective presentations I ever saw was done by a fifth grade class which had taken the poem "I Hear America Singing" by Walt Whitman, which they had been studying as a part of a social studies unit, and turned it into a performance for parents. The poem had been divided into sections which were recited by small groups and individuals as slides of "workers" were projected onto a screen. Staging consisted of children sitting around on the stage, some on stools, others on chairs, some sitting on the floor. A tape of patriotic music was played as an opening and at the closing of the recitation. Quick, easy, exciting theater!

Physical Education

Explore the movements your young actors will need on stage. Practice walks of characters of various types and ages.

Move like animals. Create the elements of nature such as wind and rain in motion.

Learn dances that might later be integrated into a play or other type of performance.

Seasonal and Holiday Programs

Dramatize a celebration from your own culture or the culture of another group or country. This might be seasonal such as the first day of Spring or Groundhog's Day; a political event such as the inauguration of a new President/Prime Minister or Independence Day; or a religious holiday such as Christmas or Easter.

Part 1

Getting Ready

Select a Play
Choose a play which is appropriate for the age and maturity of your students.
Think about...
- how much time you have to give to the play
- how much dialogue and action the play contains
- whether the play fits your needs in terms of topic, length, and difficulty in staging
- how many individual and group speaking parts it contains

If you find a play that seems appropriate for your students except for one long speaking part, invite in a "guest performer" from an older class.

If you have 30 students and the plays you are eager to do contain parts for five, consider doing a couple of short plays plus several poems on a related topic.

Prepare the Children
Keep the time between beginning to practice the play and giving the performance at a minimum, especially for younger students. Too much lead time provides opportunities for chaos and disorder plus declining interest.

Establish rules for practice times. Being quiet while other actors are speaking, standing still and quiet backstage while waiting to go on, and staying in character are all difficult for young children. These need to be practiced as well as speaking lines and moving on stage.

Have extra help when you are practicing on stage to help with the children, curtains, music, etc. This help can be parents, volunteers, or reliable older students.

Once parts have been assigned, send copies home so parents can help children begin to learn their parts. Plan short periods of time during the day to hear children say their parts. Pair them up to help each other.

Once children have become familiar with their speaking parts, begin working on moving on stage. If possible, practice on the actual area where the play will be presented. If not, mark off an area the same size and shape as the stage area for practicing moving about.

Be sure students have several opportunities to practice on stage with the sets in place and props on hand. They will not need to be in costume every time, but they should have the opportunity to practice at least once or twice wearing any costume element that might create a problem (masks, long robes, beards, crowns, etc.).

Costumes and Props

Take advantage of clothing and items you already have around the classroom, at home, or can borrow from friends, relations, fellow teachers, generous strangers. Simply adding a hat, scarf, etc., plus a bit of face make-up can take care of many situations. If you do find it necessary to make costumes, let your students help as much as possible (this will vary greatly depending on the age of your class), then call on parents. You can almost always find a few parents who are happy to help in this way. When the play is over, save the costumes for future productions - once you've helped make 72 elf costumes, you never want to repeat the activity.

headbands

hats and scarves

make-up

old clothes

creative use of classroom props

CRACKERS

costumes

Scenery

The same applies to building sets and providing props. Use items you have available at school (moveable bulletin boards, screens, room dividers, tables, etc.), then start collecting and building. Guide your students to make as much as possible, then call on outside help. Large cardboard boxes can be transformed into almost anything. Use furniture as the base of a large cardboard form such as a house front. Make wood or tri-wall easel stands to hold up smaller cardboard structures.

The addition of something special such as a potted plant "tree," real sheaves of wheat, an actual rocking chair, etc., can give your staging a professional look.

Lights and Music

Your play can be fine without the addition of any special elements such as extra lighting, music, and sound effects. The most important element to your audience is the children themselves. Adding special lights isn't necessary to most elementary school performances, but you do need to have enough light on stage for your young actors to be seen.

Music can be added using the children's own voices, live piano music provided by a student or parent volunteer, or music recorded on tape. Appoint a very reliable student or adult to be sure the music is turned off and on at the appropriate times. You must allow extra time in rehearsals for any added elements such as music.

Sound effects can be added either live or on tape.
Again, allow time for practicing this added element.

Slide Shows

Combining slides of your students along with a recitation is one variety of performance that works well even with young students.

One of the best winter performances I ever did with first graders consisted of their sitting on the front of the stage reciting "The Night Before Christmas" which they had memorized, as we showed slides of them in costume depicting scenes from the poem.

If you decide to do this type of program, give yourself enough lead time. Here is a general list of steps you might follow:

1. Select the poem you plan to recite and begin working with your students for a short period each day to memorize the poem. Send copies home for additional practice. Recite the poem together until everyone is comfortable with the words and can project clearly.

2. Plan the scenes you will photograph with your students. Involve them as much as possible in painting backdrops, making costumes, and gathering props. Call on outside help for the items you cannot find or make in class.

3. You need to allow plenty of time to get your slides taken and developed. Take slide photographs of each scene from the poem. Be sure each child is represented in the slides in some way.

If you don't feel you can do an adequate job of taking the slides, call on friends and family. You are bound to find an eager photographer among the bunch.

4. Organize the slides in order, then begin reciting the poem along with the slides. Be prepared the night of the performance with spare bulbs for the slide projector, then sit back and enjoy the performance. The audience will love it.

Part 2

Headbands for Quick and Easy Play Activities

You can make dramatic play a frequent part of your class program using these headband patterns and a few easily gathered props to act out familiar stories and poems in your classroom. The plays can be for the enjoyment of your own students or several can be put together to create a performance for other classes or for parents.

The stories suggested in this chapter are repetitive folktales, fables and rhymes. Children are already familiar with these stories, but it helps to share several versions of each story before acting out.

Steps:
1. Read or tell one or more versions of the story to your class.

2. Talk about what they can say and do to act out a role in the story.

3. Do it many times, letting different people have a chance to be the main characters.

Play Activities in Part 2

Henny Penny 16
Characters:
Henny Penny Ducky Lucky
Turkey Lurkey
Cocky Lockey
Foxy Loxy

The Three Little Kittens 17
Characters:
Mother Cat
Kitten #1, #2, #3

The City Mouse and Country Mouse 18
Characters:
Country Mouse
City Mouse
Cat

The Gingerbread Man 19
Characters:
Gingerbread Man
Old Woman
Old Man
Cow
Farmers
Fox
Children

The Three Little Pigs 20
Characters:
First Little Pig
Second Little Pig
Third Little Pig
Wolf

The Lion and the Mouse 21
Characters:
Lion
Mouse
Hunters

Caps for Sale 22
Characters:
Salesman
Many Monkeys

The Three Billy Goats Gruff 23
Characters:
Little Billy Goat
Middle-sized Billy Goat
Big Billy Goat
Troll

The Little Red Hen 24
Characters:
Little Red Hen
Dog
Duck
Mouse
Chicks

Goldilocks and the Three Bears 25
Characters:
Goldilocks
Papa Bear
Mama Bear
Baby Bear

Headband Patterns 26-45

Getting Ready

Room Set-up

The headbands can be used to represent characters in stories other than those we suggest here. You may even want to try creating original plays with some of these characters. Children have wonderfully creative imaginations when given a chance.

Find a corner of the room to leave samples of the headbands for "free play." This will become a favorite area for your students.

How to Make Headbands

1. Color and cut out the headband parts.
2. Cut two strips of construction paper (2 1/2" x 11" or 6.5 x 28 cm).
3. Paste the construction paper strips to the sides of the headband pattern.
4. Fit the headband on the student. How big is their head? Overlap the paper strips to a comfortable spot and staple in place.

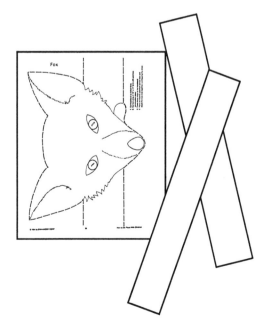

Henny Penny

The misadventures of Henny Penny make a delightful story for dramatic play. Children enjoy the repetitive language and can remember the simple plot for re-telling in their own words. There are enough parts for several children to participate at one time. Staging is simple and a headband becomes all the costume anyone needs.

The characters sit in chairs in the order of their appearance in the play. Henny Penny moves her chair forward as she speaks. Each player follows Henny Penny and moves up into line as they enter the story.
A sheet is laid over a table to create Foxy Loxy's cave.

1. Henny Penny

2. Ducky Lucky

3. Turkey Lurkey

4. Cocky Lockey

5. Foxy Loxy

The Three Little Kittens

Those careless little kittens learn their lesson when they miss out on Mother's delicious pie until they locate the missing mittens.

Everyone sits in a circle to help recite the poem. Mother stands to one side in her apron. The kittens sit in chairs, standing when they recite their parts.

1. Mother Cat

   apron

2. Kitten #1, #2, #3

   mittens on page 33

The City Mouse and the Country Mouse

The little country mouse discovers that city life isn't so perfect when he meets a hungry cat. This is an opportunity for three "stars" to perform, while the rest of the class practices audience skills.

The country is two chairs and a basket of country food (nuts, corn, etc.). The city is a table with dishes of "goodies" set to the other side of your play area. The cat hides under the table until needed. City Mouse visits the Country Mouse, trying out his food and simple way of life. He invites the Country Mouse to visit his city. They walk over to the "city" and try the food, only to be chased by the hungry cat. Country Mouse returns home.

1. Country Mouse

   add the straw hat on **page 33**

2. City Mouse

   add the small hat on **page 33**

3. Cat

The Gingerbread Man

The refrain from this story is the perfect way to get your shyer students started. By increasing the number of cows, farmers, and children you can provide roles for as many students as you wish. Let everyone repeat the refrain as the Gingerbread Man runs.

The characters sit in chairs in the order of their appearance. The Gingerbread Man starts at the left. He runs around the chairs as the chase takes place. At the end of the row, the fox holds a sheet of blue "water." The Gingerbread Man stands behind the fox. Both bend lower and lower as the water gets deeper. Finally, the Gingerbread Man disappears behind a smiling fox!

1. Gingerbread Man

2. Old Woman
   scarf and
   apron

3. Old Man
   old cap
   or hat

4. Cow

5. Farmers
   straw hats
   and kerchiefs

6. Fox

7. Children
   pretend to be playing
   ball and jumprope

How to Do Plays With Children

The Three Little Pigs

The little pigs learn that you need a sturdy house if there is a hungry wolf in your neighborhood!

Children stand in a circle to make the walls of the house. Two stand to form the doorway. (They will hold straw, sticks or bricks to represent each type of house.) The pigs sit in the house until needed. Wolf "blows the house down." The walls sit down and the wolf chases one little pig around outside. The walls stand up to form the next house and the pig runs inside. After the wolf tries to blow down the brick house, two children join hands to form the chimney. The wolf comes through and then falls down dead.

1. First little pig

   sign with #1
   broomstraw in a
   kerchief on a stick

2. Second little pig

   sign with #2
   sticks in a
   kerchief on a stick

3. Third little pig

   sign with #3
   a brick in a
   kerchief on a stick

4. Wolf

How to Do Plays With Children

The Lion and the Mouse

Small size doesn't keep a brave little mouse from helping a large lion. Children can take turns being the fierce lion and the helpful mouse.

The action moves from one side of the room to the other as the play progresses. The mouse stumbles across the sleeping lion. After he releases the mouse (who runs away), the lion walks across the room onto the net (sheet, tablecloth, etc.) and covers himself so he looks "captured." The mouse comes along and unwraps the lion as the rescue occurs.

1. Lion    2. Mouse

3. Hunters
   Wear hats and carry their "net"

Caps for Sale

Mischievous little monkeys can't resist all the salesman's hats. They also can't resist playing "Monkey See, Monkey Do" when he tries to get the hats back.

The monkeys sit in a semi-circle with their heads down as the salesman comes along looking for a tree to rest under. He is wearing (or carrying) many hats. He sits down and goes to sleep. The monkeys sit up; then they sneak out one at a time to steal the hats. The salesman wakes up, discovers his hats are gone, and tries to get them back from the monkeys.

1. Salesman wearing a large stack of hats

2. Monkey (any number)

Caps For Sale is a delightful story by Esphyr Slobodkina, Young Scott Books, © 1940.

The Three Billy Goats Gruff

The grass looks greener on the other side of the bridge, so off go the hungry goats. Everyone can help make the "clip-clop" of the goats' feet. Watch out for the troll!

A table and two chairs become a bridge from one meadow to the other. The troll hides under the table until the goats begin to prance across. You may want to choose your goats according to size. Put signs around the necks of the goats.

1. Little Billy Goat

   sign—Little

2. Middle-sized Billy Goat

   sign—Middle

3. Big Billy Goat

   sign—Big

4. Troll

 How to Do Plays With Children

The Little Red Hen

Little Red Hen gives up on the lazy dog, mouse and duck. She does all the work herself. Then she gives the delicious bread to her baby chicks as the other animals look on. You might want to try making real homemade bread with your class!

All the little chicks sit in a semi-circle as the action takes place. They can peep occasionally. The dog, duck, and mouse rest on rugs (towels) while the hen goes about her business. Have a bag for her to take to the mill and a table with a bowl and bread pan for her to use when baking her bread.

1. Little Red Hen

apron

2. Dog

3. Duck

4. Mouse

5. Chicks

 How to Do Plays With Children

Goldilocks and the Three Bears

One naughty little girl, an empty house, and three returning bears add up to an exciting story to act out in your classroom.

The children sit in a circle to become the walls of the house. A space is left for the door, and two children stand, holding hands, to form the window through which Goldilocks escapes. Line up a table with three bowls, three chairs, and three beds (towels on the floor). Then let the action begin.

1. Goldilocks

2. Papa Bear

   add a bow tie

3. Mama Bear

   a shawl and an apron

4. Baby Bear

   a teddy bear

Duck

1. Cut headband on dotted lines.
2. Cut two strips 2 1/2" x 11" (6.5 x 28 cm) from construction paper.
3. Paste these strips to the headband.
4. Place on head to establish correct size and staple the two ends together, overlapping the strips.

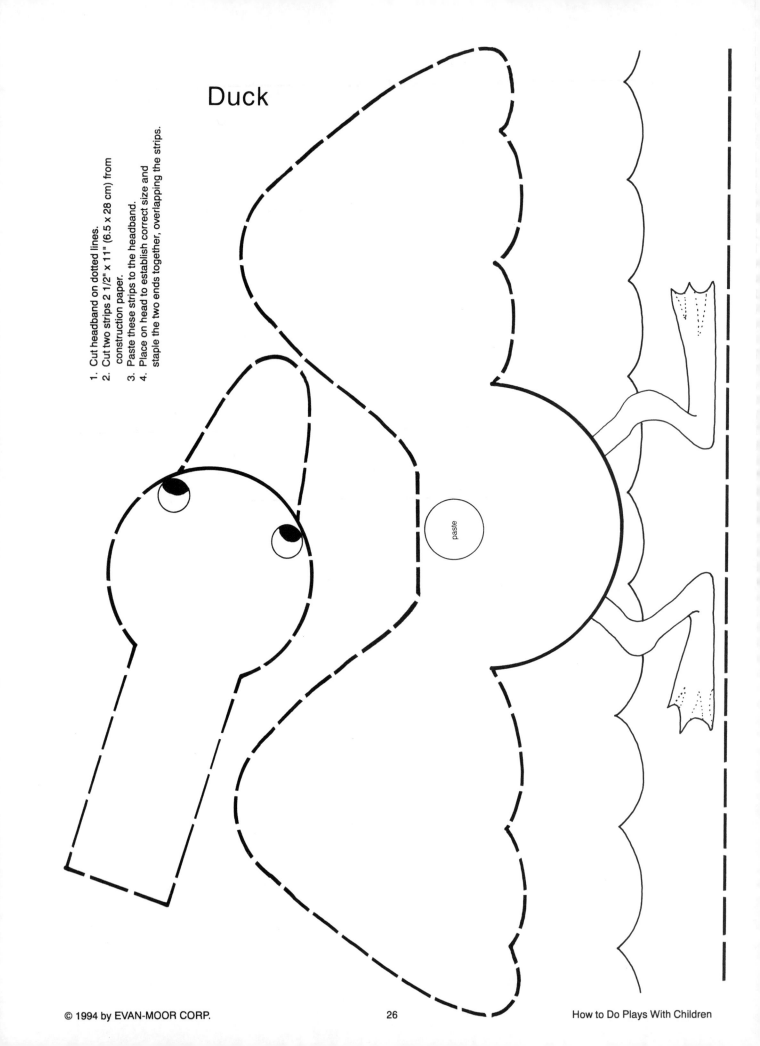

paste

26

How to Do Plays With Children

Hen

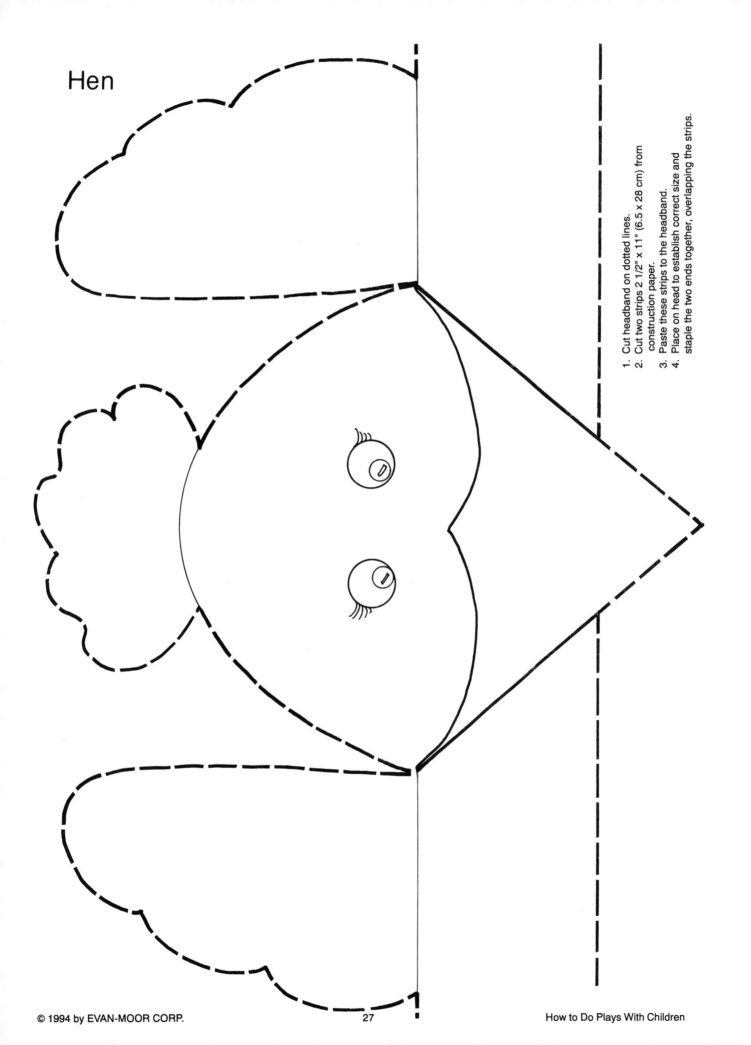

1. Cut headband on dotted lines.
2. Cut two strips 2 1/2" x 11" (6.5 x 28 cm) from construction paper.
3. Paste these strips to the headband.
4. Place on head to establish correct size and staple the two ends together, overlapping the strips.

How to Do Plays With Children

Rooster

1. Cut headband on dotted lines.
2. Cut two strips 2 1/2" x 11" (6.5 x 28 cm) from construction paper.
3. Paste these strips to the headband.
4. Place on head to establish correct size and staple the two ends together, overlapping the strips.

paste

Turkey

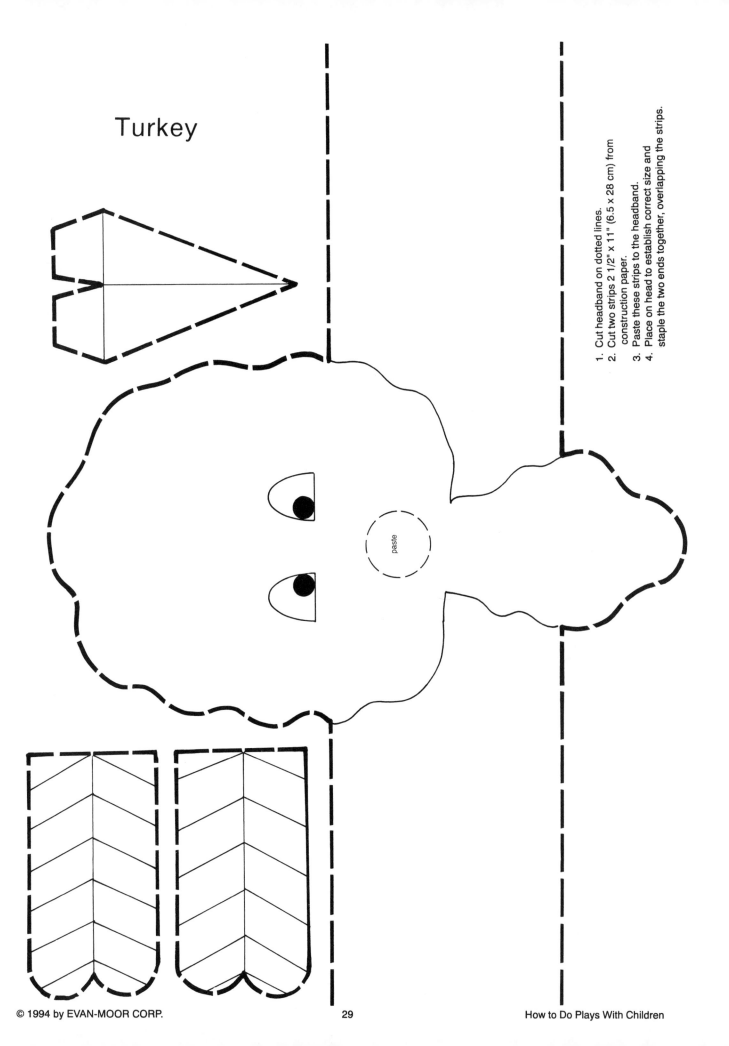

paste

1. Cut headband on dotted lines.
2. Cut two strips 2 1/2" x 11" (6.5 x 28 cm) from construction paper.
3. Paste these strips to the headband.
4. Place on head to establish correct size and staple the two ends together, overlapping the strips.

How to Do Plays With Children

Fox

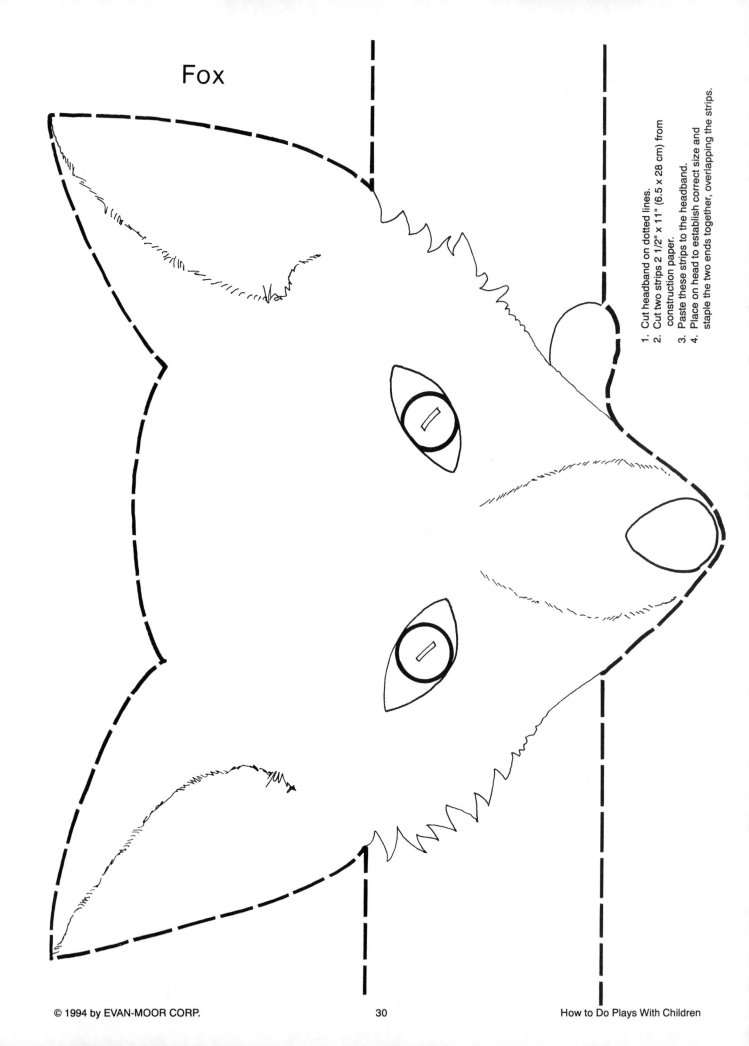

1. Cut headband on dotted lines.
2. Cut two strips 2 1/2" x 11" (6.5 x 28 cm) from construction paper.
3. Paste these strips to the headband.
4. Place on head to establish correct size and staple the two ends together, overlapping the strips.

         How to Do Plays With Children

Kitten

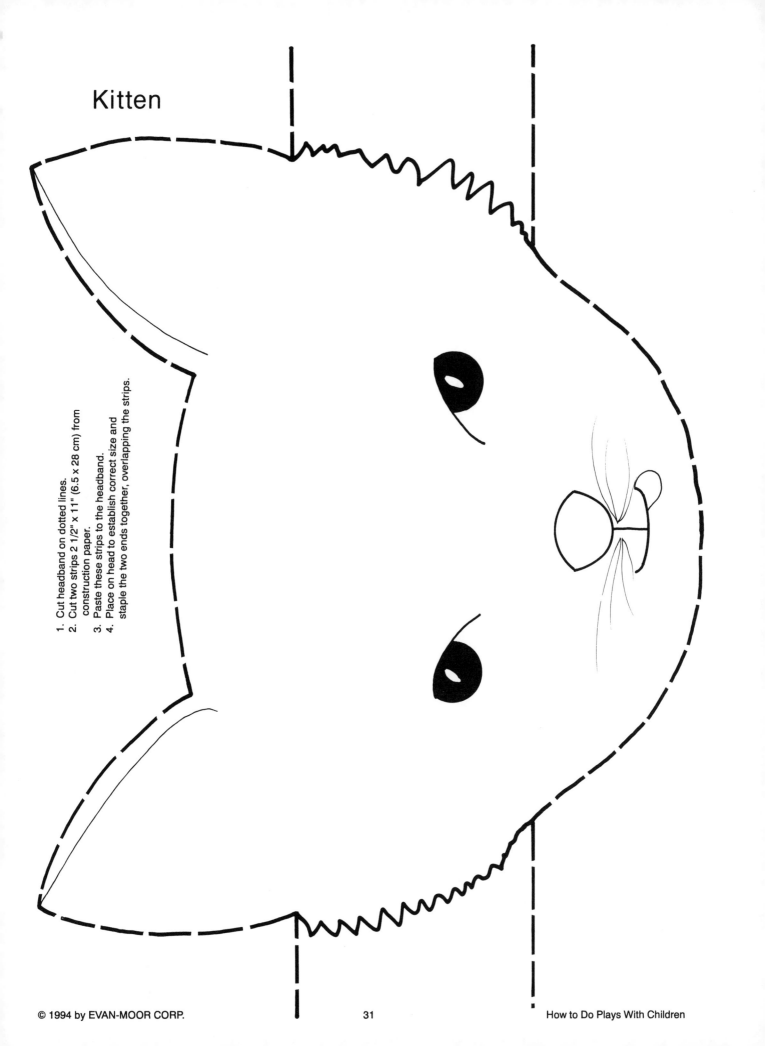

1. Cut headband on dotted lines.
2. Cut two strips 2 1/2" x 11" (6.5 x 28 cm) from construction paper.
3. Paste these strips to the headband.
4. Place on head to establish correct size and staple the two ends together, overlapping the strips.

How to Do Plays With Children

Mouse

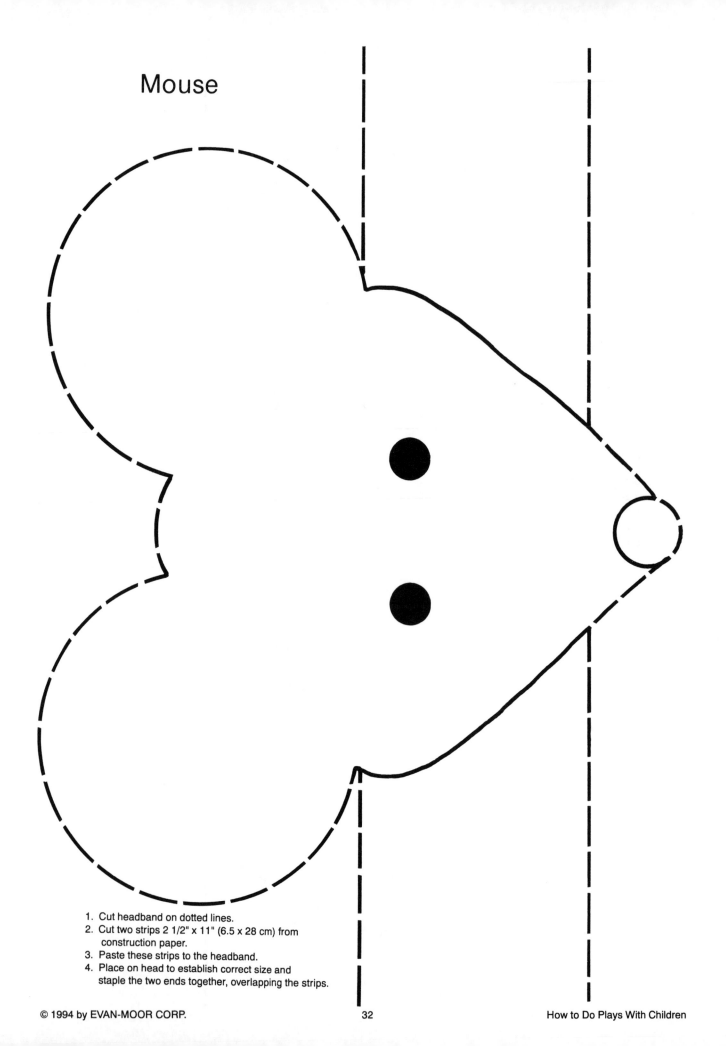

1. Cut headband on dotted lines.
2. Cut two strips 2 1/2" x 11" (6.5 x 28 cm) from
   construction paper.
3. Paste these strips to the headband.
4. Place on head to establish correct size and
   staple the two ends together, overlapping the strips.

How to Do Plays With Children

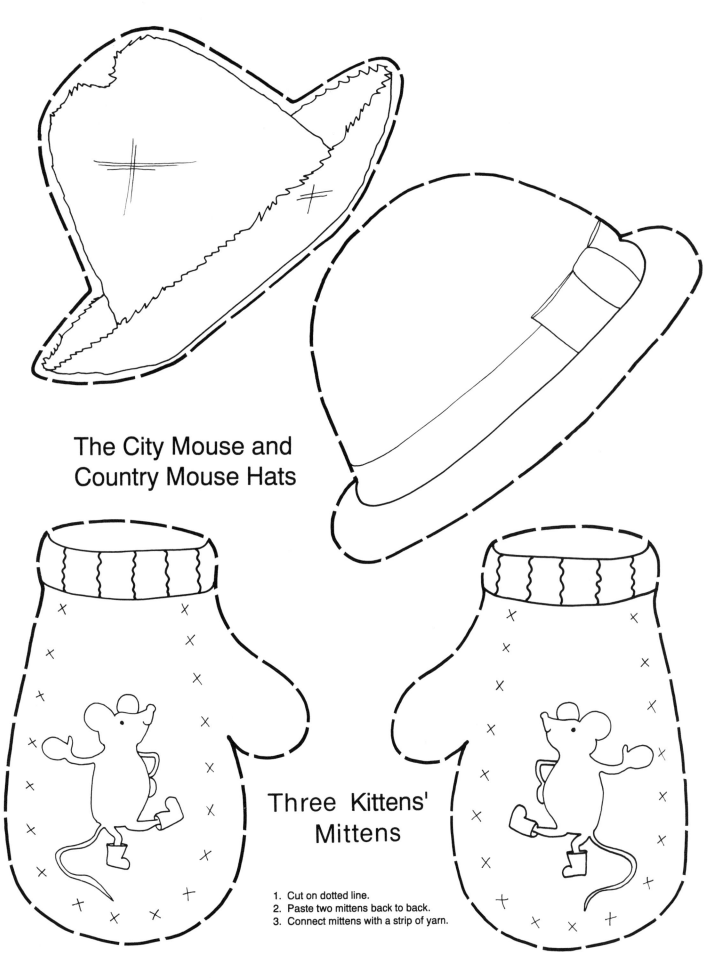

The City Mouse and
Country Mouse Hats

Three Kittens'
Mittens

1. Cut on dotted line.
2. Paste two mittens back to back.
3. Connect mittens with a strip of yarn.

33

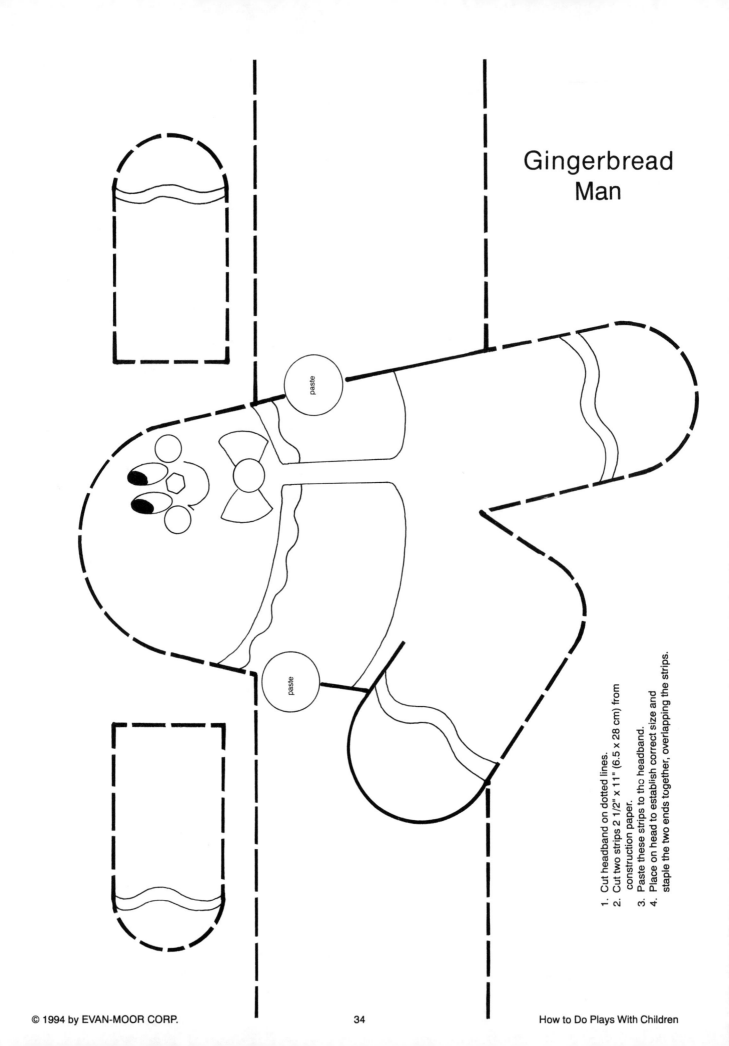

Gingerbread Man

paste

paste

1. Cut headband on dotted lines.
2. Cut two strips 2 1/2" x 11" (6.5 x 28 cm) from construction paper.
3. Paste these strips to the headband.
4. Place on head to establish correct size and staple the two ends together, overlapping the strips.

How to Do Plays With Children

Cow

paste

paste

3. Paste these strips to the headband.
4. Place on head to establish correct size and staple the two ends together, overlapping the strips.

1. Cut headband on dotted lines.
2. Cut two strips 2 1/2" x 11" (6.5 x 28 cm) from construction paper.

How to Do Plays With Children

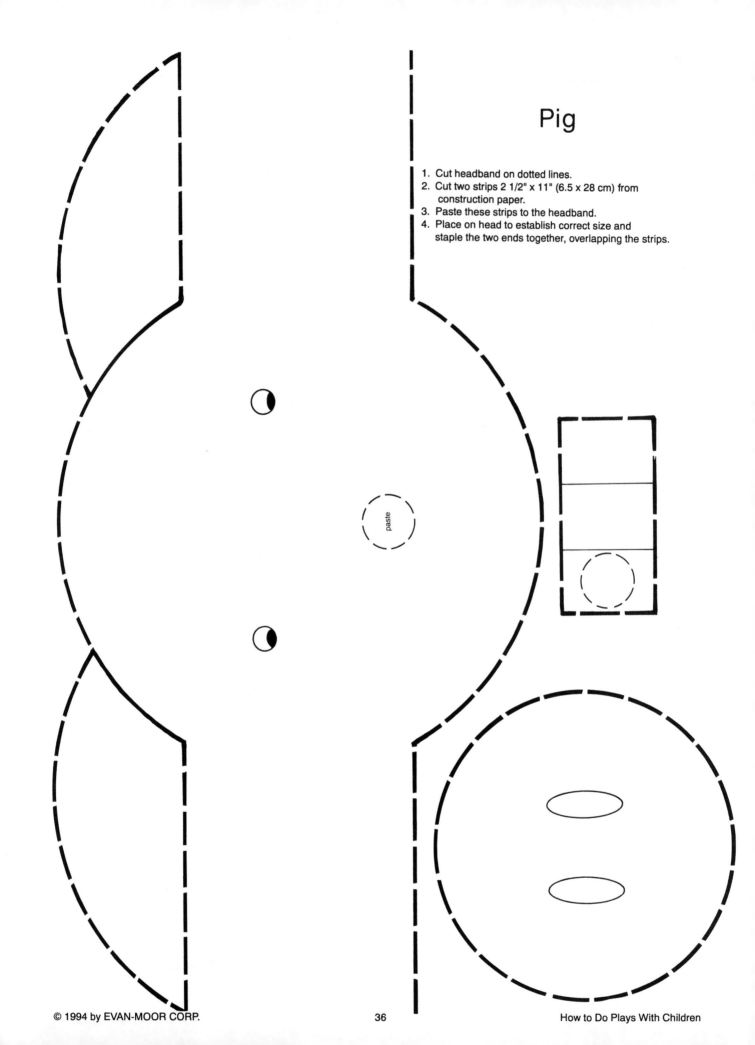

Pig

1. Cut headband on dotted lines.
2. Cut two strips 2 1/2" x 11" (6.5 x 28 cm) from construction paper.
3. Paste these strips to the headband.
4. Place on head to establish correct size and staple the two ends together, overlapping the strips.

paste

How to Do Plays With Children

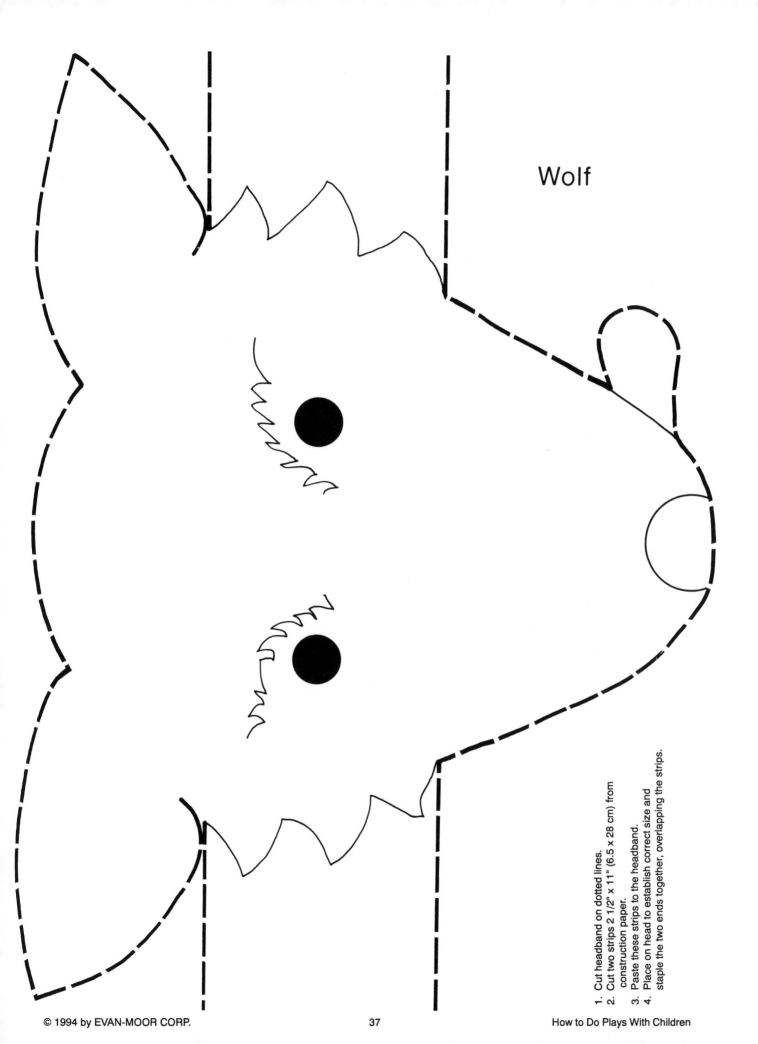

Wolf

1. Cut headband on dotted lines.
2. Cut two strips 2 1/2" x 11" (6.5 x 28 cm) from construction paper.
3. Paste these strips to the headband.
4. Place on head to establish correct size and staple the two ends together, overlapping the strips.

How to Do Plays With Children

Lion

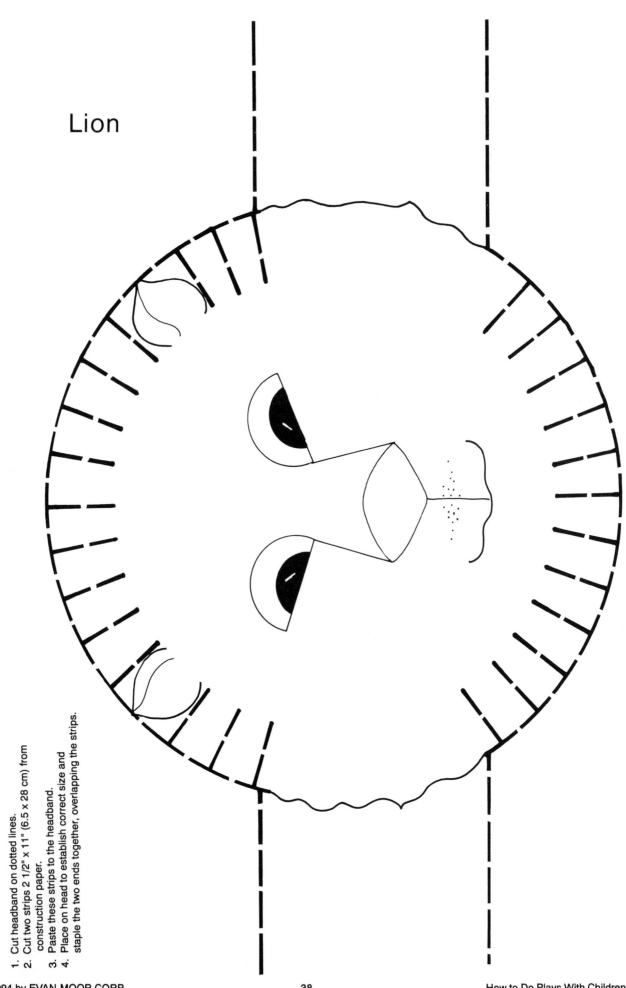

1. Cut headband on dotted lines.
2. Cut two strips 2 1/2" x 11" (6.5 x 28 cm) from construction paper.
3. Paste these strips to the headband.
4. Place on head to establish correct size and staple the two ends together, overlapping the strips.

                   How to Do Plays With Children

Monkey

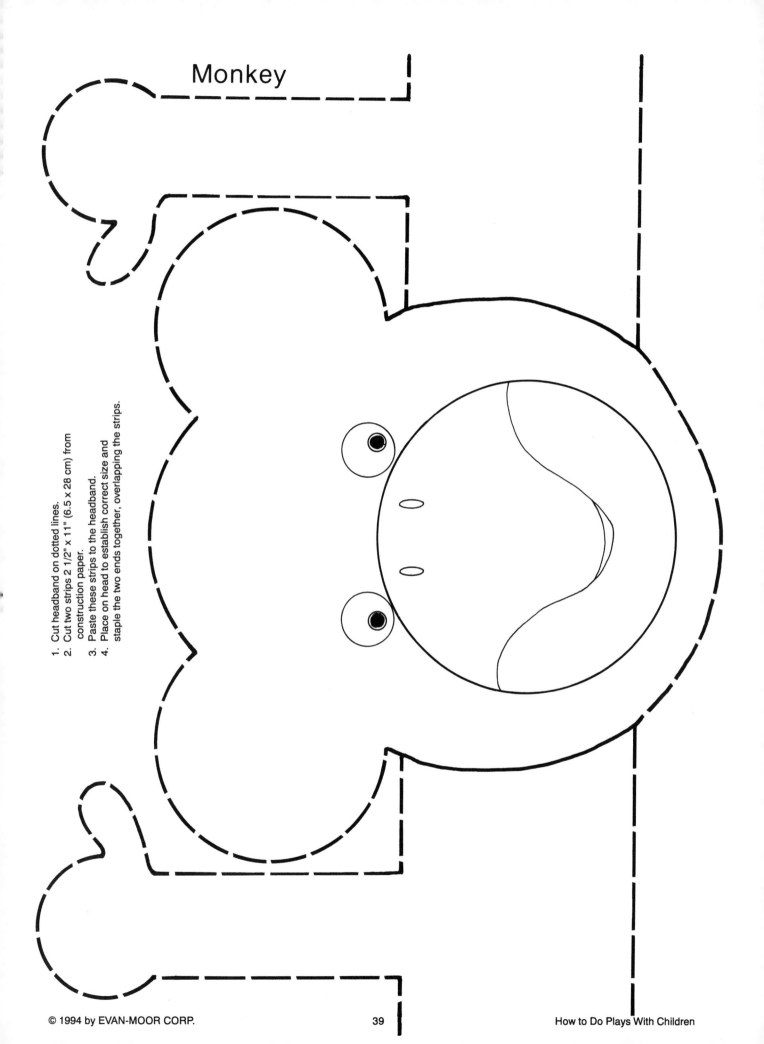

1. Cut headband on dotted lines.
2. Cut two strips 2 1/2" x 11" (6.5 x 28 cm) from construction paper.
3. Paste these strips to the headband.
4. Place on head to establish correct size and staple the two ends together, overlapping the strips.

How to Do Plays With Children

Goat

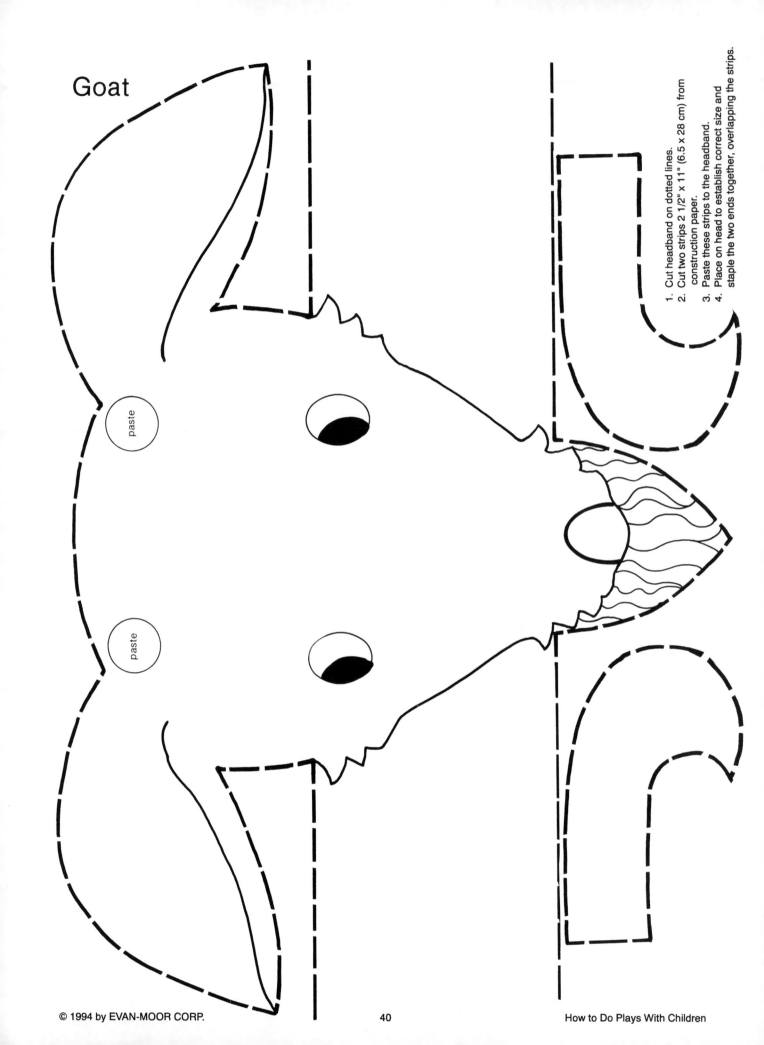

1. Cut headband on dotted lines.
2. Cut two strips 2 1/2" x 11" (6.5 x 28 cm) from construction paper.
3. Paste these strips to the headband.
4. Place on head to establish correct size and staple the two ends together, overlapping the strips.

paste

paste

How to Do Plays With Children

Troll

1. Cut headband on dotted lines.
2. Cut two strips 2 1/2" x 11" (6.5 x 28 cm) from construction paper.
3. Paste these strips to the headband.
4. Place on head to establish correct size and staple the two ends together, overlapping the strips.

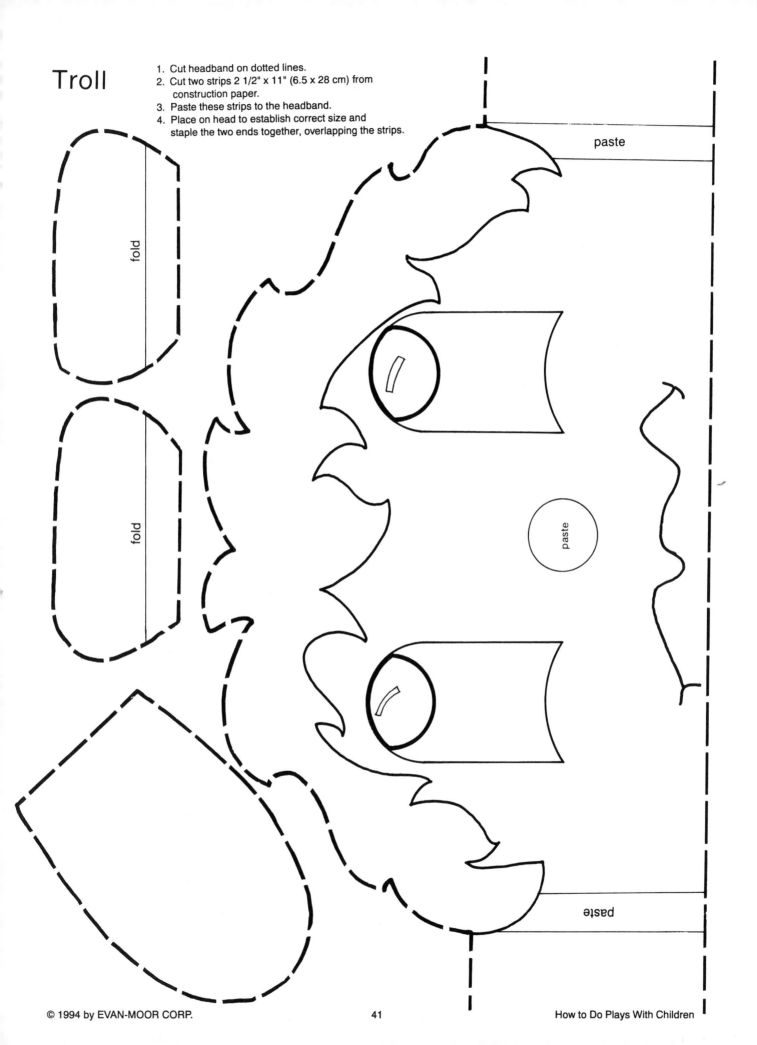

41

Dog

fold

fold

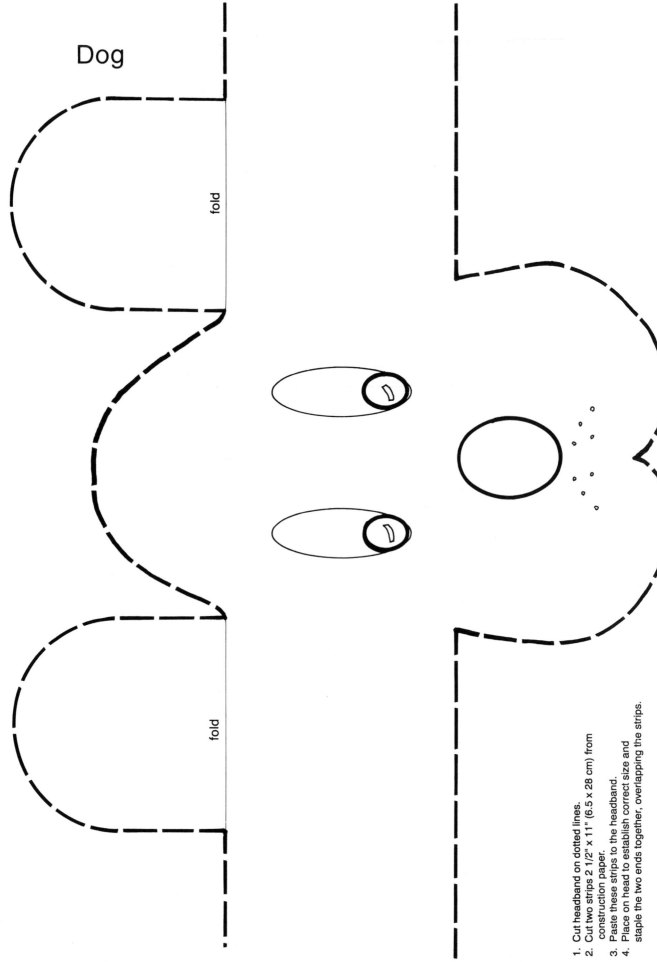

1. Cut headband on dotted lines.
2. Cut two strips 2 1/2" x 11" (6.5 x 28 cm) from construction paper.
3. Paste these strips to the headband.
4. Place on head to establish correct size and staple the two ends together, overlapping the strips.

How to Do Plays With Children

Chick

1. Cut headband on dotted lines.
2. Cut two strips 2 1/2" x 11" (6.5 x 28 cm) from construction paper.
3. Paste these strips to the headband.
4. Place on head to establish correct size and staple the two ends together, overlapping the strips.

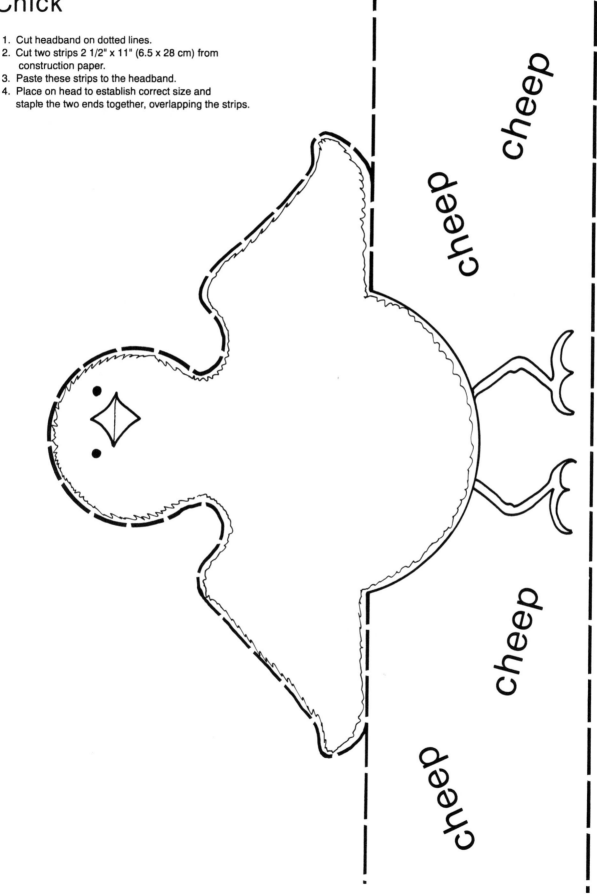

43   How to Do Plays With Children

Goldilocks

1. Cut headband on dotted lines.
2. Cut two strips 2 1/2" x 11" (6.5 x 28 cm) from construction paper.
3. Paste these strips to the headband.
4. Place on head to establish correct size and staple the two ends together, overlapping the strips.

fold

fold

Color both sides of Goldilocks' hair and fold forward, and curl on a pencil.

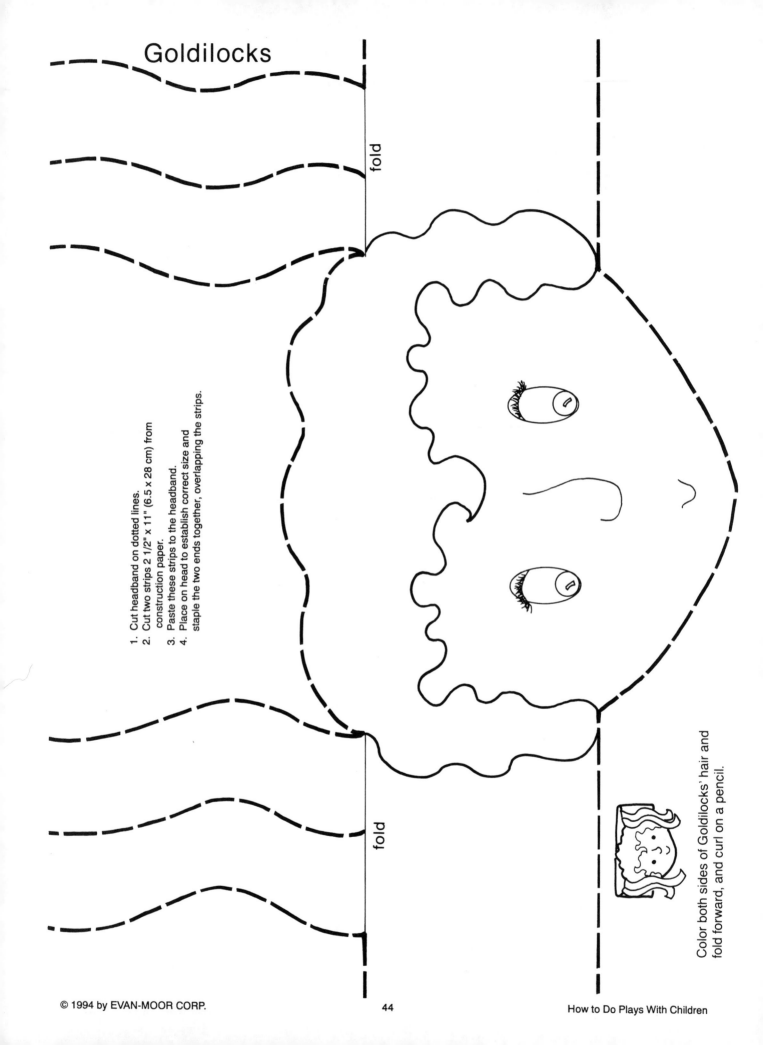

How to Do Plays With Children

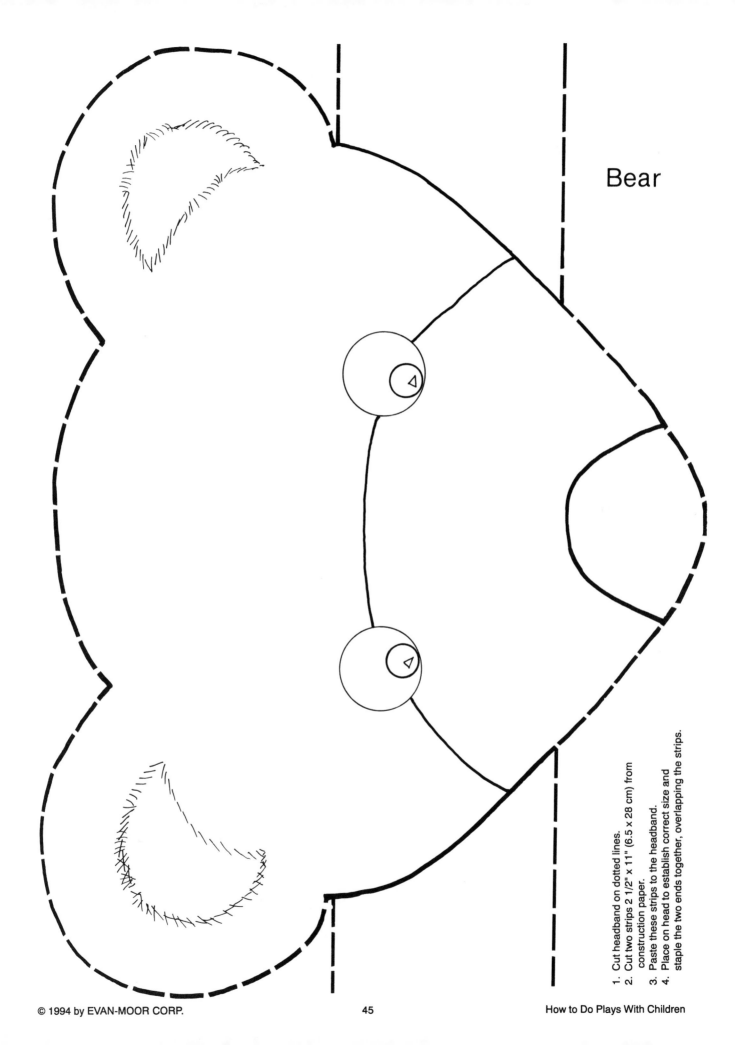

Bear

1. Cut headband on dotted lines.
2. Cut two strips 2 1/2" x 11" (6.5 x 28 cm) from construction paper.
3. Paste these strips to the headband.
4. Place on head to establish correct size and staple the two ends together, overlapping the strips.

How to Do Plays With Children

Please Come to School
and
Share
Our Play Activities

day and date

time

place

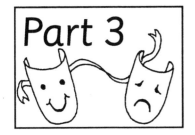
Part 3

Rhyming Plays

Fun for Everyone

Students of all ages respond to the reading and hearing of rhyming verses. These plays have been written to provide your students with plays that are easy to memorize and fun to share with an audience.

These scripts are ideal for young performers but they have also been successfully produced by older students to share with primary students.

The plays have been constructed so that some parts can be played by groups of students performing in unison; in this way you can accomodate all the students in your class. Some students will have many lines, some students only a few.

Rhyming Plays
in
Part 3

Mother Goose's Goose is Loose (Nursery Rhymes) 49

The Little Red Hen 79

Goldilocks and the Three Bears 108

A Flea on Santa's Tree? (a Christmas Play) 134

Spring Starts Here! (Groundhog's Day) 159

A Rhyming Play
Fun for Everyone

Mother Goose's Goose is Loose

by Leslie Tryon

Scenery	50
Characters and Costumes	52
Props	54
Script	55
Take-Home Practice Script	61
Invitation	65
Play Program	66
Goose Puzzle	67
Mystery Character	78

How to Do Plays with Children

Scenery

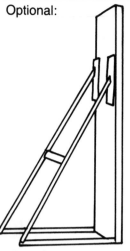

For free-standing set, support puzzle backing easel style.

Children enter holding their puzzle piece behind them. They recite for Mother Goose and then put their puzzle piece in place, out of view of Mother Goose.

Page stands in one place throughout and directs the children, one at a time, to recite for Mother Goose. He or she just points when directing.

How to Do Plays with Children

Tape (double stick) puzzle pieces directly onto the wall. Make a puzzle grid on the wall with tape outlining areas where children will place pieces. Number the wall grid.

10	2	9	3	7
1	5	6	4	8

Puzzle backboard is drawn on butcher paper. Number each section to match the puzzle pieces.

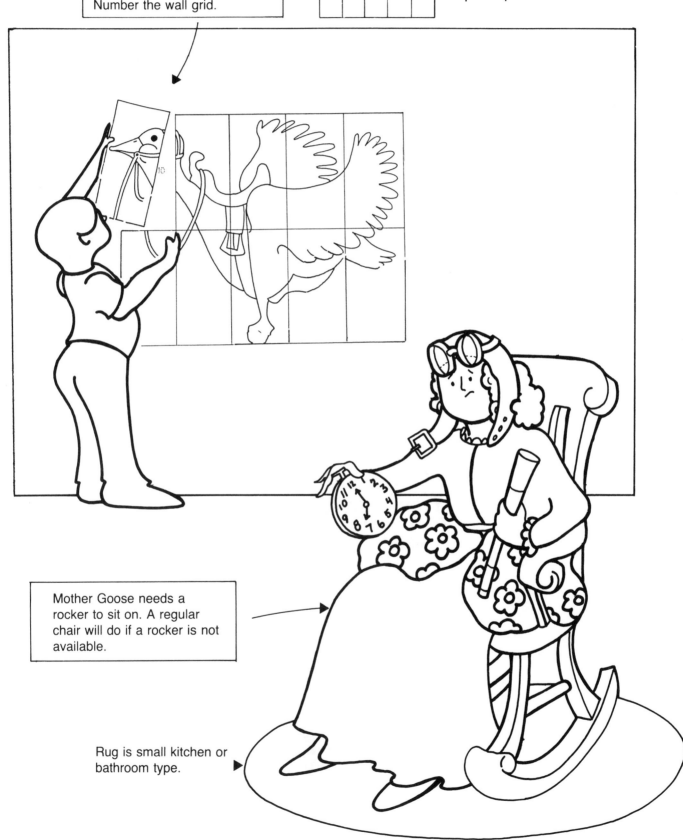

Mother Goose needs a rocker to sit on. A regular chair will do if a rocker is not available.

Rug is small kitchen or bathroom type.

Characters and Costumes

Mother Goose

The part of Mother Goose will be the most fun for the children if played by the teacher or an older student. The children love the fact that they know all along what is happening, and Mother Goose is the last to know.

A blouse with ruffles will do well, worn with a long, dark skirt (if available). Considering the humorous theme, Mother Goose could even get away with wearing pants.

Side bustles are made from flowered pillowcases, stuffed with batting and attached to a ribbon that ties in the back. Swimming goggles will work for the flying goggles. She wears a long scarf tied around her neck. If you don't know someone who will let you borrow their World War II aviator helmet, wear a bathing cap.

　　　　　　　　　　　　　　How to Do Plays with Children

Any large margarine container will do for the hat. Glue or staple the chin strap to the container and trim with the same ribbon you used on the pants. The page should wear a plain turtleneck T-shirt.

Glue or sew ribbon to the side seams of the page's pants.

The boys and girls who recite the rhymes (any number up to 30), should wear dark trousers and skirts, and plain light-colored T-shirts.

Props

Telescope
A piece of black construction paper rolled into a flared tube. Tape the seam and glue to the paper towel tube.

Scroll
Staple construction paper to two dowels and roll up. If dowels are not available, use paper-towel rolls.

Watch
Reproduce on card stock. Staple a ribbon to the top of watch. Pin other end of ribbon to Mother Goose's waist. The watch hangs down to her side.

Paper-towel roll covered with black construction paper.

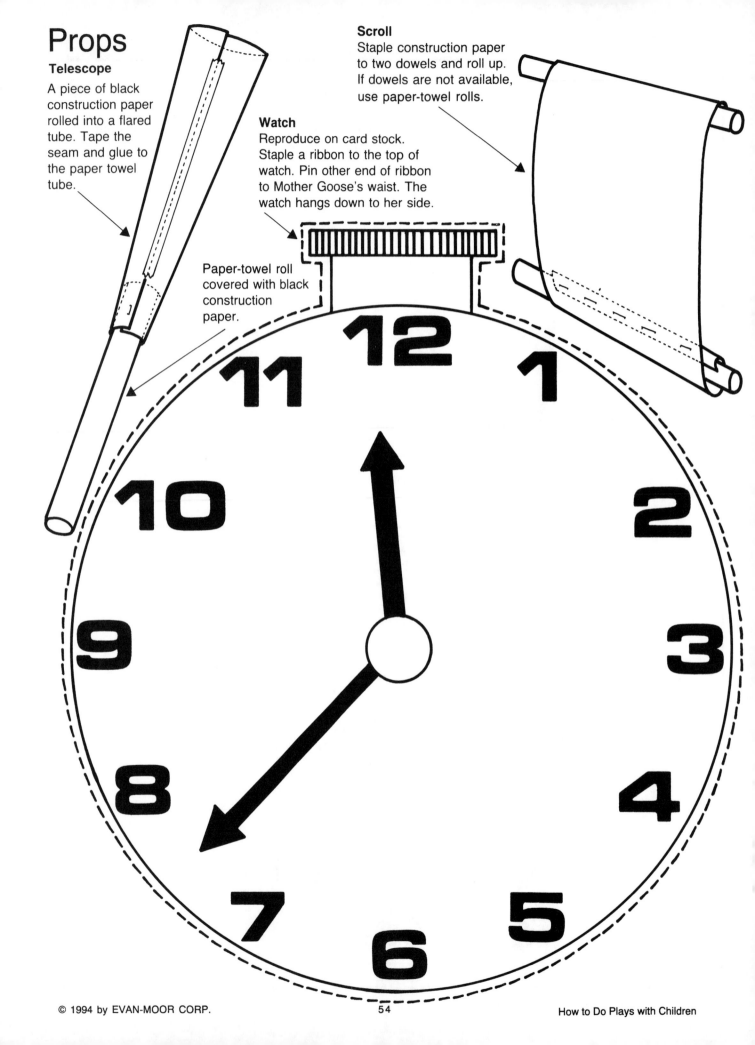

How to Do Plays with Children

Mother Goose's Goose is Loose
Script

Mother Goose:

I'm old Mother Goose,
And I'm ready to wander.
But I've looked high and low,
And I can't find my gander.

I've looked in my pocket.
I've looked in my shoe.
I've looked in the cupboard.
I've looked up the flue.

I think I need help
From my good friends of rhyme.
I'll send out a call.
I just hope it's in time.

Mother Goose stands center stage, scans the skies with her telescope and then speaks.

The page enters carrying a scroll. He stands facing the audience.

Page:

Hear Ye! Hear Ye!
I have a puzzle here.
Bring your rhymes and hurry.
Mother Goose needs help I fear.

Page "reads" to the audience. Mother Goose goes to her chair as he reads, takes off her goggles, and waits. Page exits.

Mother Goose:

The hands on my watch
Keep going around.
My goose is still gone,
And my friends can't be found.

Mother Goose looks at her watch, holding it toward the audience.

The page returns with all the children. They carry their puzzle pieces behind them.

Page:

They're here! They're here!
They've come from afar;
By horse and by camel,
By train, boat, and car.

When each child finishes placing the puzzle piece in place, he or she sits on the floor to the side and in front of Mother Goose.

How to Do Plays with Children

Mother Goose:

My goose is loose.
I'm grounded. Boo Hoo!
It's a puzzle to me,
And I need help from you.

*Mother Goose
says her lines from
her chair.*
*The page stands
between the line of children
and Mother Goose and
directs each child, in
turn, to stand before
Mother Goose and recite.*

*Children say their lines to
Mother Goose. One child in
the group holds the puzzle
piece behind his or her back.*

Girl(s) #1:

Little Miss Muffet
Sat on a tuffet,
Eating her curds and whey.

There came a big spider,
And sat down beside her,
And frightened Miss Muffet away.

*After Mother Goose says
her lines, the child with
the puzzle piece goes
to the wall grid and
puts the piece in place.
The children then go to
the side and sit on the
floor.*

*The page then directs the
next group to stand in
front of Mother Goose.*

Mother Goose:
Refrain:
*Repeat this rhyme after each of
the children's rhymes.*

Your rhyme is nice,
But what's the use?
It cannot help
Bring back my goose.

*Repeat this procedure
for each rhyme part.
Occasionally you can
have Mother Goose scan
the skies with her
telescope or look at her
watch again.*

Boy(s) #1:

Little Jack Horner
Sat in the corner,
Eating a Christmas Pie.

He put in his thumb,
And pulled out a plum
And said, "What a good boy am I!"

Mother Goose:

Your rhyme is nice,
But what's the use?
It cannot help
Bring back my goose.

Girl(s) #2:

Mary, Mary, quite contrary,
How does your garden grow?

Silver bells and cockle-shells,
And pretty maids all in a row.

Mother Goose:

Your rhyme is nice,
But what's the use?
It cannot help
Bring back my goose.

Boy(s) #2:

Little Boy Blue, come blow your horn.
The sheep's in the meadow,
The cow's in the corn.

Where's the little boy that
Looks after the sheep?
Under the haystack, fast asleep.

Mother Goose:

Your rhyme is nice,
But what's the use?
It cannot help
Bring back my goose.

Boy(s) #3:

Jack be nimble,
Jack be quick,
Jack jump over the candlestick.

Mother Goose:

Your rhyme is nice,
But what's the use?
It cannot help
Bring back my goose.

Girl(s) #3:

Old Mother Hubbard
Went to the cupboard
To give her poor dog a bone;

But when she got there,
The cupboard was bare,
And so the poor dog had none.

Mother Goose:

Your rhyme is nice,
But what's the use?
It cannot help
Bring back my goose.

Boy(s) #4:

Georgy Porgy, pudding and pie,
Kissed the girls and made them cry.
When the boys came out to play,
Georgy Porgy ran away.

Mother Goose:

Your rhyme is nice,
But what's the use?
It cannot help
Bring back my goose.

Girl(s) #4:

Three blind mice! See how they run!
They all ran after the farmer's wife,
Who cut off their tails with a carving knife.

Did you ever see such a thing in your life
As three blind mice?

Mother Goose:

Your rhyme is nice,
But what's the use?
It cannot help
Bring back my goose.

Boy(s) #5:

Jack Sprat
Could eat no fat,
His wife could eat no lean;

And so
Betwixt them both,
They licked the platter clean.

Mother Goose:

Your rhyme is nice,
But what's the use?
It cannot help
Bring back my goose.

Girl(s) #5:

There was a little girl,
Who had a little curl,
Right in the middle of her forehead.

When she was good,
She was very, very good,
And when she was bad she was horrid.

Mother Goose:

I'm old Mother Goose
And I'm stuck on the ground,
While that gander of mine
Is up playing around.

*Mother Goose gets up
and walks over to the
group of children as
she says her lines.*

*Mother Goose needs to
remember to keep her
back to the puzzle
at all times.*

Chorus:

Your puzzle is solved,
So please don't despair.
Your goose is behind you
Not up in the air.

Put on your goggles,
Your scarf, and get set
To take off and fly
On your favorite pet.

When the children say "your goose is behind you" they all point at once to the puzzle.

Mother Goose turns, sees the puzzle for the first time, and registers surprise.

Old Mother Goose, when
She wanted to wander,
Would ride through the air
On a very fine gander.

The End

For the final stanza the children get up and say their lines to the audience. Mother Goose puts her goggles back on, tosses her scarf over her shoulder (with flair), and strikes a pose in front of her goose.

Mother Goose:

I'm old Mother Goose,
And I'm ready to wander.
But I've looked high and low,
And I can't find my gander.

I've looked in my pocket.
I've looked in my shoe.
I've looked in the cupboard.
I've looked up the flue.

I think I need help
From my good friends of rhyme.
I'll send out a call.
I just hope it's in time.

The hands on my watch
Keep going around.
My goose is still gone,
And my friends can't be found.

My goose is loose.
I'm grounded. Boo Hoo!
It's a puzzle to me,
And I need help from you.

Your rhyme is nice,
But what's the use?
It cannot help
Bring back my goose.

I'm old Mother Goose
And I'm stuck on the ground,
While that gander of mine
Is up playing around.

Chorus:

Your puzzle is solved,
So please don't despair.
Your goose is behind you
Not up in the air.

Put on your goggles,
Your scarf, and get set
To take off and fly
On your favorite pet.

Old Mother Goose, when
She wanted to wander,
Would ride through the air
On a very fine gander.

Take-Home Practice Script

Dear Parent - Please help your child learn these lines for a class play. Thank you.

Boy(s) #1:

Little Jack Horner
Sat in the corner,
Eating a Christmas Pie.

He put in his thumb,
And pulled out a plum,
And said, "What a good boy am I!"

Take-Home Practice Script

Dear Parent - Please help your child learn these lines for a class play. Thank you.

Girl(s) #1:

Little Miss Muffet
Sat on a tuffet,
Eating her curds and whey.

There came a big spider,
And sat down beside her,
And frightened Miss Muffet away.

Take-Home Practice Script

Dear Parent - Please help your child learn these lines for a class play. Thank you.

Boy(s) #2:

Little Boy Blue, come blow your horn.
The sheep's in the meadow,
The cow's in the corn.

Where's the little boy that
Looks after the sheep?
Under the haystack, fast asleep.

Take-Home Practice Script

Dear Parent - Please help your child learn these lines for a class play. Thank you.

Girl(s) #2:

Mary, Mary, quite contrary,
How does your garden grow?

Silver bells and cockle-shells,
And pretty maids all in a row.

Take-Home Practice Script
Dear Parent - Please help your child learn these lines for a class play. Thank you.

Boy(s) #3:

Jack be nimble,
Jack be quick,
Jack jump over the candlestick.

Take-Home Practice Script
Dear Parent - Please help your child learn these lines for a class play. Thank you.

Girl(s) #3:

Old Mother Hubbard
Went to the cupboard
To give her poor dog a bone;

But when she got there,
The cupboard was bare,
And so the poor dog had none.

Take-Home Practice Script
Dear Parent - Please help your child learn these lines for a class play. Thank you.

Boy(s) #4:

Georgy Porgy, pudding and pie,
Kissed the girls and made them cry.
When the boys came out to play,
Georgy Porgy ran away.

Take-Home Practice Script
Dear Parent - Please help your child learn these lines for a class play. Thank you.

Girl(s) #4:

Three blind mice! See how they run!
They all ran after the farmer's wife,
Who cut off their tails with a carving knife.

Did you ever see such a thing in your life
As three blind mice?

Take-Home Practice Script
Dear Parent - Please help your child learn
these lines for a class play. Thank you.

Take-Home Practice Script
Dear Parent - Please help your child learn
these lines for a class play. Thank you.

Boy(s) #5:

Jack Sprat
Could eat no fat,
His wife could eat no lean;

And so
Betwixt them both,
They licked the platter clean.

Girl(s) #5:

There was a little girl,
Who had a little curl,
Right in the middle of her forehead.

When she was good,
She was very, very good,
And when she was bad she was horrid.

Take-Home Practice Script
Dear Parent - Please help your child learn
these lines for a class play. Thank you.

Page:

Hear Ye! Hear Ye!
I have a puzzle here.
Bring your rhymes and hurry.
Mother Goose needs help I fear.

They're here! They're here!
They've come from afar;
By horse and by camel,
By train, boat, and car.

class:

presents the play

Mother Goose's
Goose is Loose

date:

time:

place:

Please join us!

 How to Do Plays with Children

Mother Goose's Goose is Loose

Mother Goose: _____

Page: _____

Mother Goose Rhymes Recited By:

Goose Puzzle

Reproduce the Goose Puzzle pieces on the following pages. Trim on the dotted lines. Use these pieces during the play to reconstruct Mother Goose's missing goose behind her back. You may enlarge the pieces if you want the puzzle to be seen by a large group.

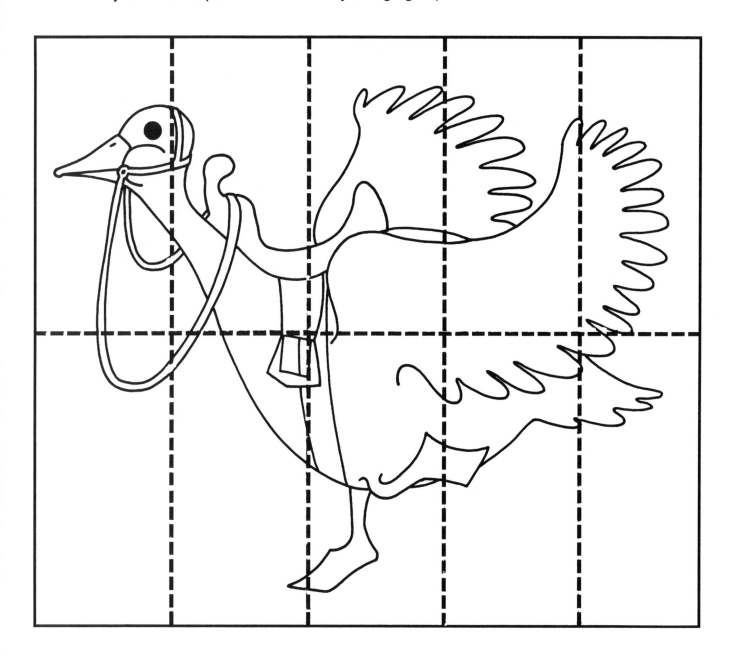

Mother Goose Puzzle

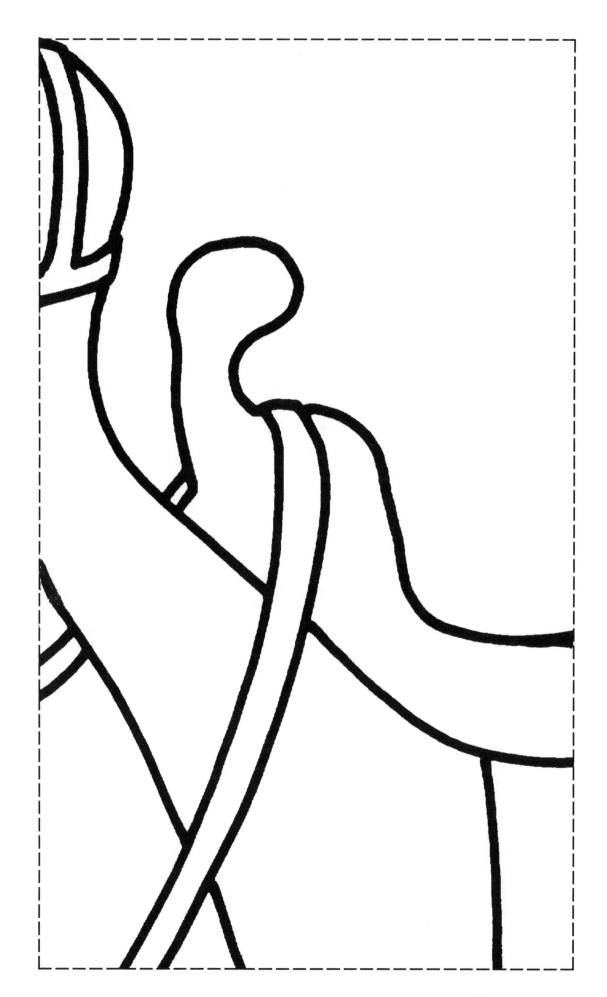

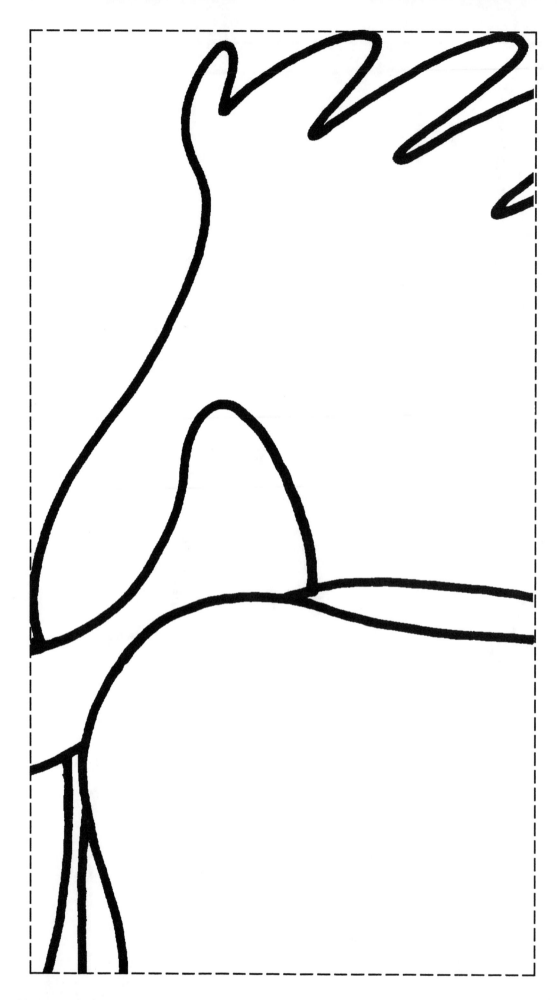

How to Do Plays with Children

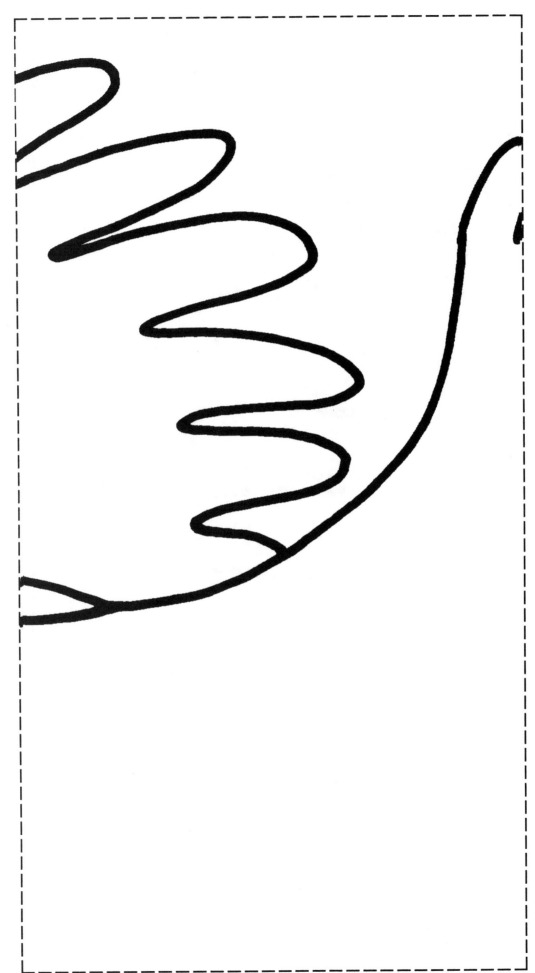

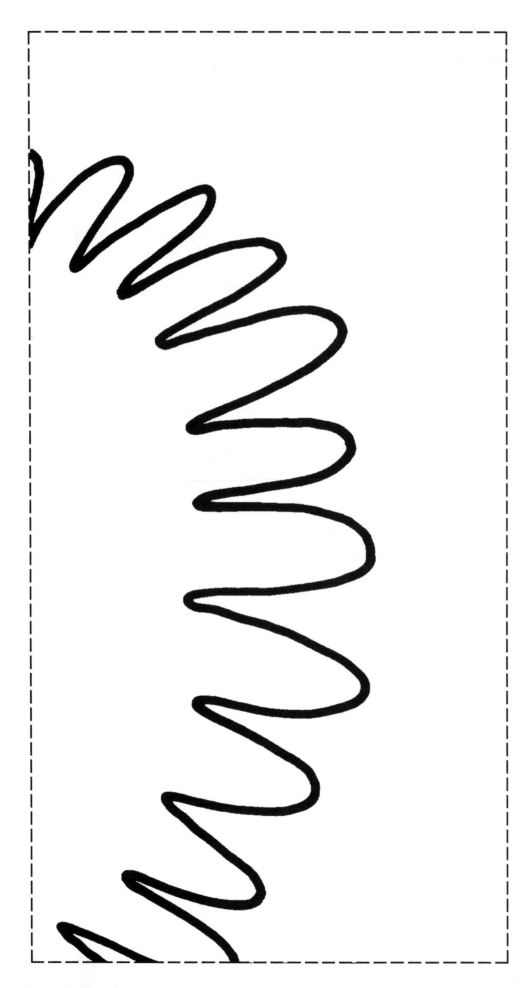

How to Do Plays with Children

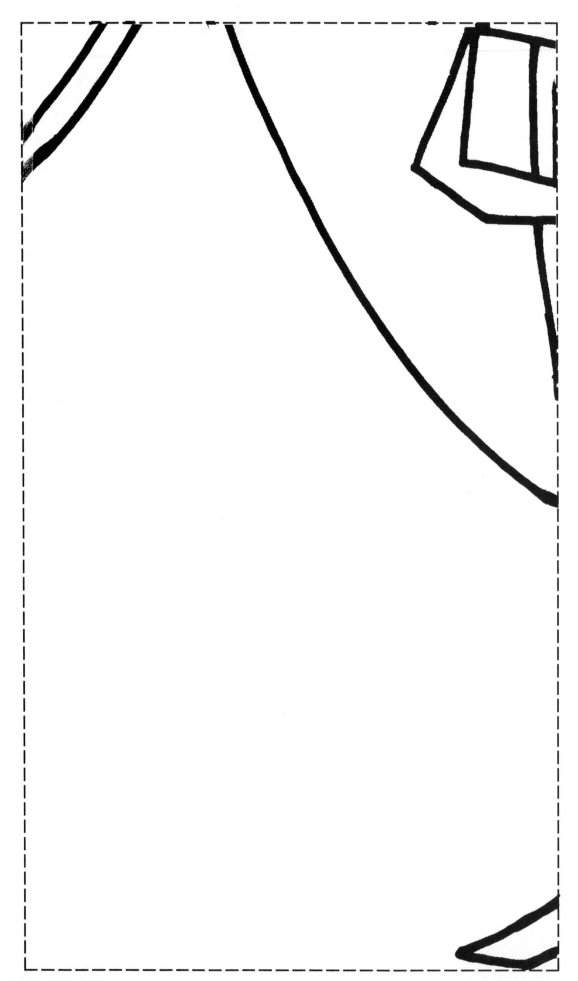

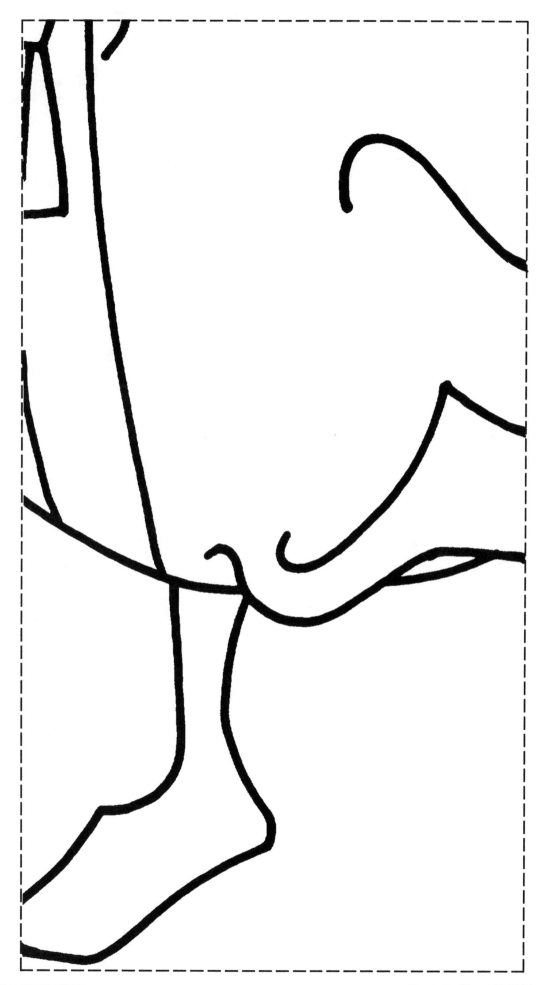

How to Do Plays with Children

How to Do Plays with Children

How to Do Plays with Children

The Mystery Character

1. Cut on the dotted lines.
2. Paste the pieces together on a piece of paper.
3. Who is this famous character?

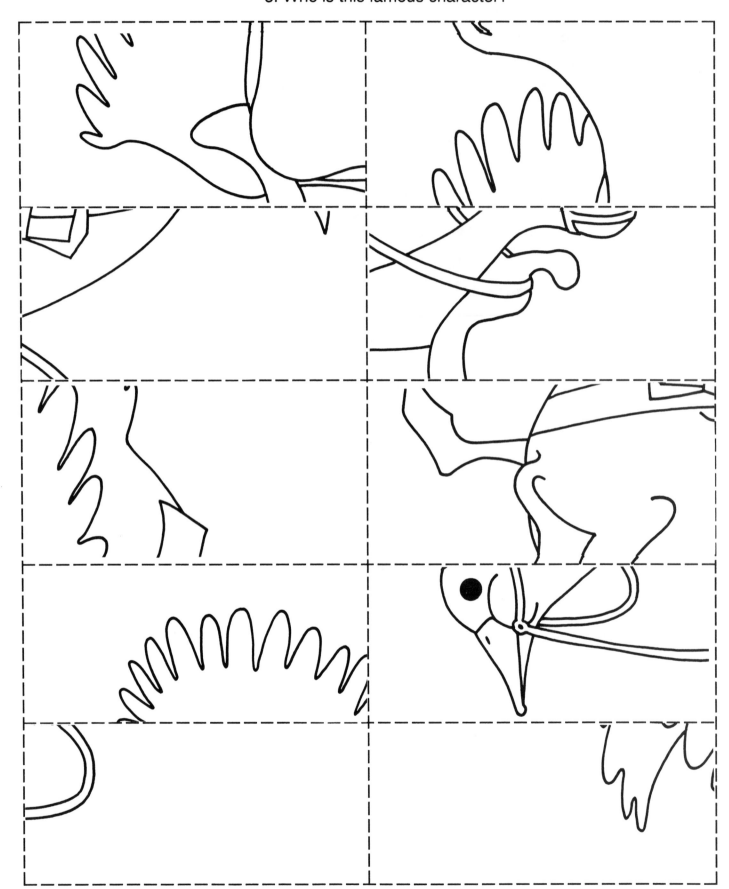

78   How to Do Plays with Children

The Little Red Hen

by Leslie Tryon

Scenery	80
Costumes	82
Props	84
Masks	86
"Match" Activity	94
Script	95
Take-Home Practice Script	102
Invitation	106
Play Program	107

How to Do Plays with Children

Scenery

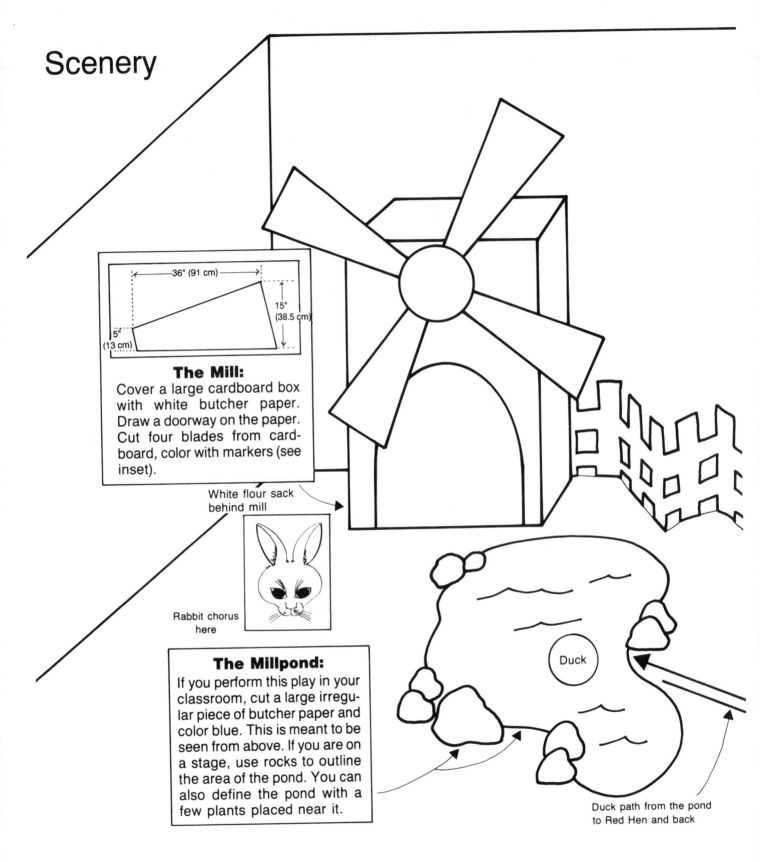

36" (91 cm)

15" (38.5 cm)

5" (13 cm)

The Mill:
Cover a large cardboard box with white butcher paper. Draw a doorway on the paper. Cut four blades from cardboard, color with markers (see inset).

White flour sack behind mill

Rabbit chorus here

The Millpond:
If you perform this play in your classroom, cut a large irregular piece of butcher paper and color blue. This is meant to be seen from above. If you are on a stage, use rocks to outline the area of the pond. You can also define the pond with a few plants placed near it.

Duck

Duck path from the pond to Red Hen and back

Cow chorus here

Napping cat

How to Do Plays with Children

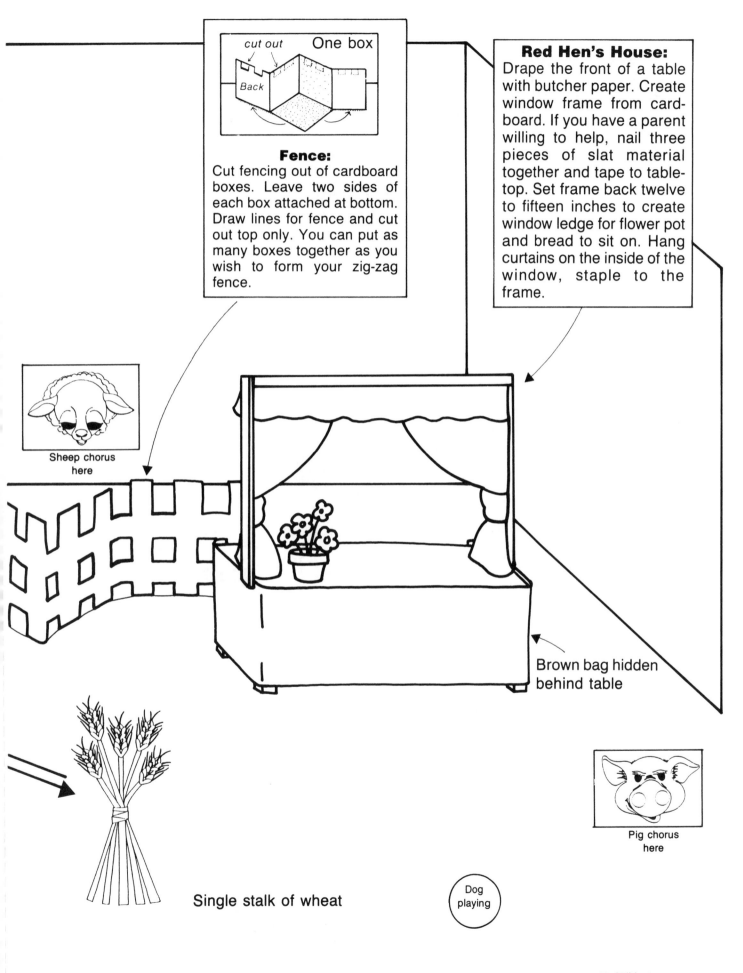

One box

cut out

Back

Fence:

Cut fencing out of cardboard boxes. Leave two sides of each box attached at bottom. Draw lines for fence and cut out top only. You can put as many boxes together as you wish to form your zig-zag fence.

Red Hen's House:

Drape the front of a table with butcher paper. Create window frame from cardboard. If you have a parent willing to help, nail three pieces of slat material together and tape to tabletop. Set frame back twelve to fifteen inches to create window ledge for flower pot and bread to sit on. Hang curtains on the inside of the window, staple to the frame.

Sheep chorus here

Brown bag hidden behind table

Pig chorus here

Single stalk of wheat

Dog playing

How to Do Plays with Children

Costumes

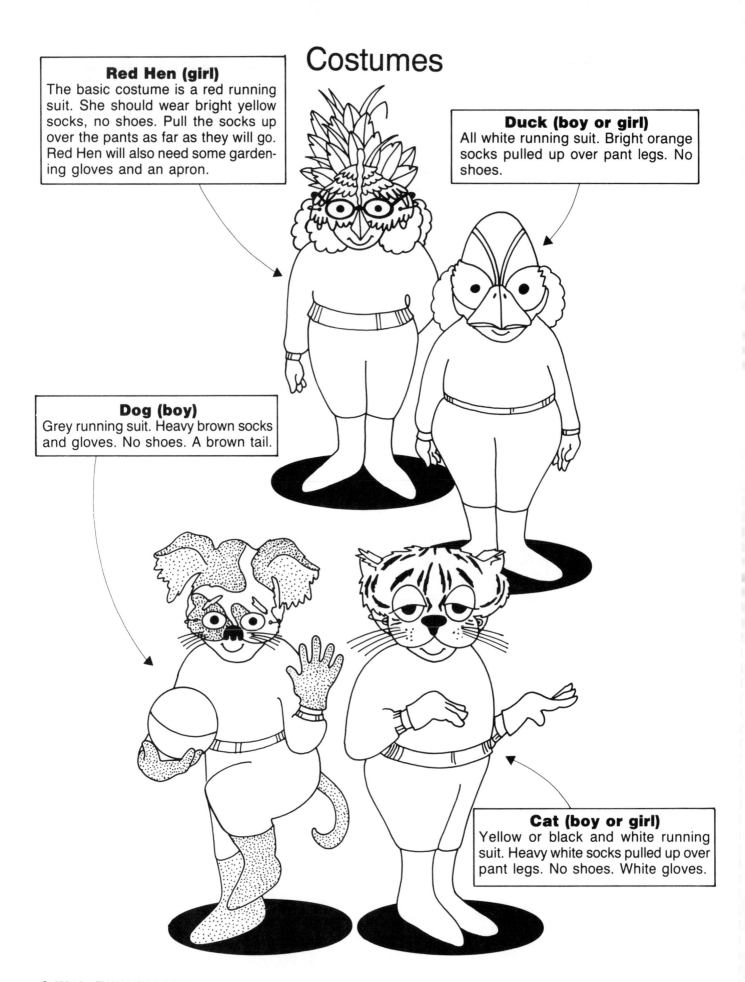

Red Hen (girl)
The basic costume is a red running suit. She should wear bright yellow socks, no shoes. Pull the socks up over the pants as far as they will go. Red Hen will also need some gardening gloves and an apron.

Duck (boy or girl)
All white running suit. Bright orange socks pulled up over pant legs. No shoes.

Dog (boy)
Grey running suit. Heavy brown socks and gloves. No shoes. A brown tail.

Cat (boy or girl)
Yellow or black and white running suit. Heavy white socks pulled up over pant legs. No shoes. White gloves.

How to Do Plays with Children

Cows

Chorus:
Boys and girls of the chorus should all wear very dark, black if possible, clothes. Their mask should be their only color.

Sheep

Rabbits

Pigs

Props

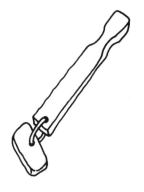

Flail

Ball

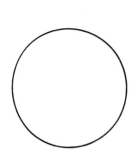

Stick

Sock

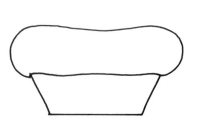

Bread pan with bread

White bag (pillowcase) with FLOUR written on it

Flower pot with flowers

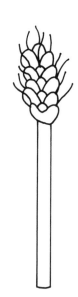

Stalk of wheat

Brown bag for wheat

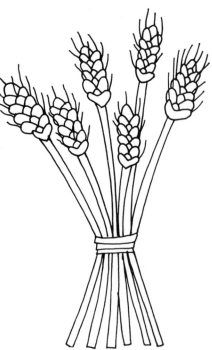

Stalks of wheat

How to Do Plays with Children

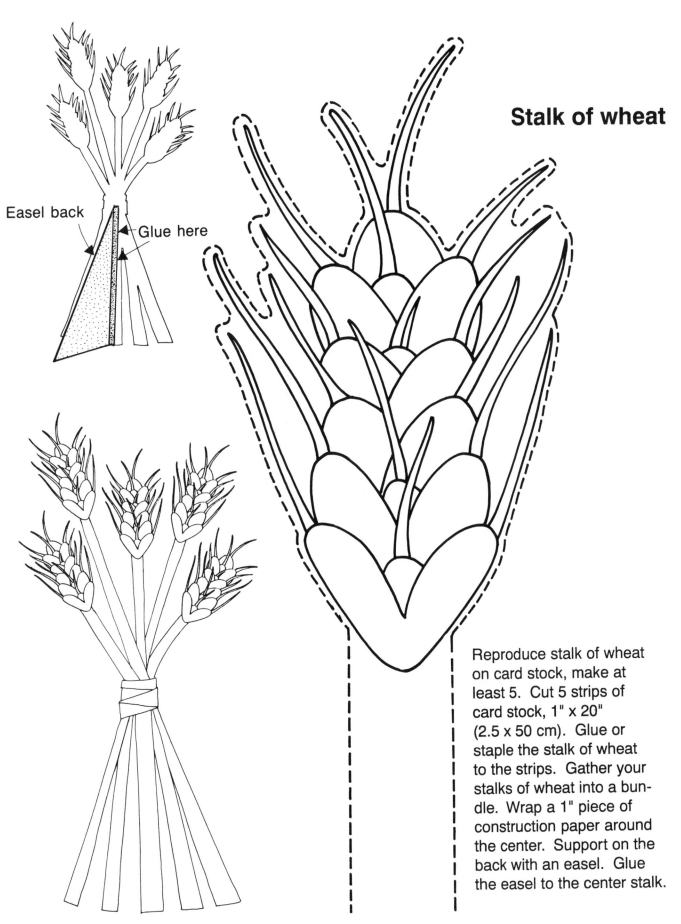

Easel back

Glue here

Stalk of wheat

Reproduce stalk of wheat
on card stock, make at
least 5. Cut 5 strips of
card stock, 1" x 20"
(2.5 x 50 cm). Glue or
staple the stalk of wheat
to the strips. Gather your
stalks of wheat into a bun-
dle. Wrap a 1" piece of
construction paper around
the center. Support on the
back with an easel. Glue
the easel to the center stalk.

How to Do Plays with Children

Red Hen Mask

Cut out

Cut out

1. Reproduce mask on card stock.
2. Cut mask on dotted lines.
3. Cut eye holes with Exacto knife and punch holes for ribbon.
4. Color with markers.

5. Tie a knot in one end of two 14" (35.5 cm) pieces of ribbon. Thread through punched holes.
6. Fold mask forward on outside of punched holes to keep mask facing forward.

How to Do Plays with Children

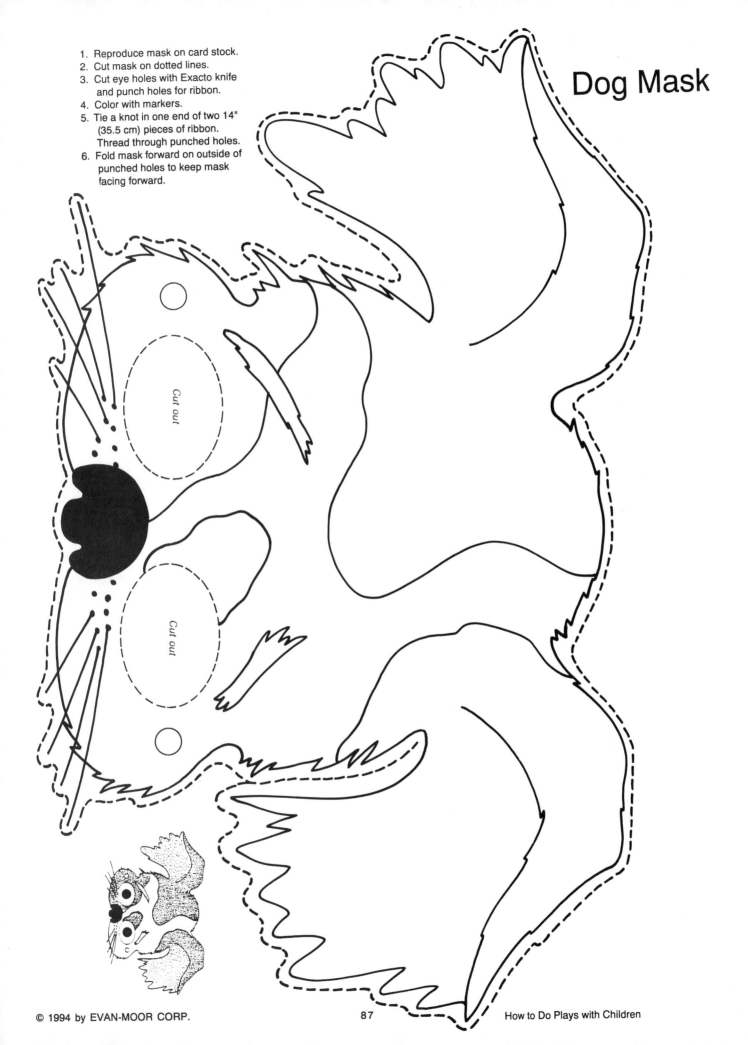

1. Reproduce mask on card stock.
2. Cut mask on dotted lines.
3. Cut eye holes with Exacto knife and punch holes for ribbon.
4. Color with markers.
5. Tie a knot in one end of two 14" (35.5 cm) pieces of ribbon. Thread through punched holes.
6. Fold mask forward on outside of punched holes to keep mask facing forward.

Dog Mask

Cut out

Cut out

How to Do Plays with Children

Cat Mask

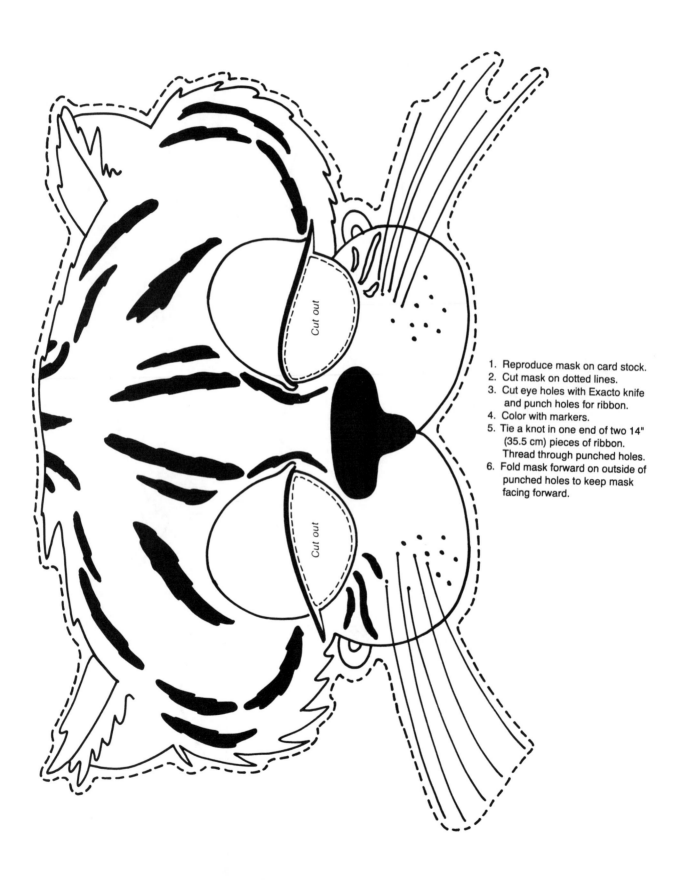

Cut out

Cut out

1. Reproduce mask on card stock.
2. Cut mask on dotted lines.
3. Cut eye holes with Exacto knife and punch holes for ribbon.
4. Color with markers.
5. Tie a knot in one end of two 14" (35.5 cm) pieces of ribbon. Thread through punched holes.
6. Fold mask forward on outside of punched holes to keep mask facing forward.

How to Do Plays with Children

Duck Mask

1. Reproduce mask on card stock.
2. Cut mask on dotted lines.
3. Cut eye holes with Exacto knife and punch holes for ribbon.
4. Color with markers.
5. Tie a knot in one end of two 14" (35.5 cm) pieces of ribbon. Thread through punched holes.
6. Fold mask forward on outside of punched holes to keep mask facing forward.

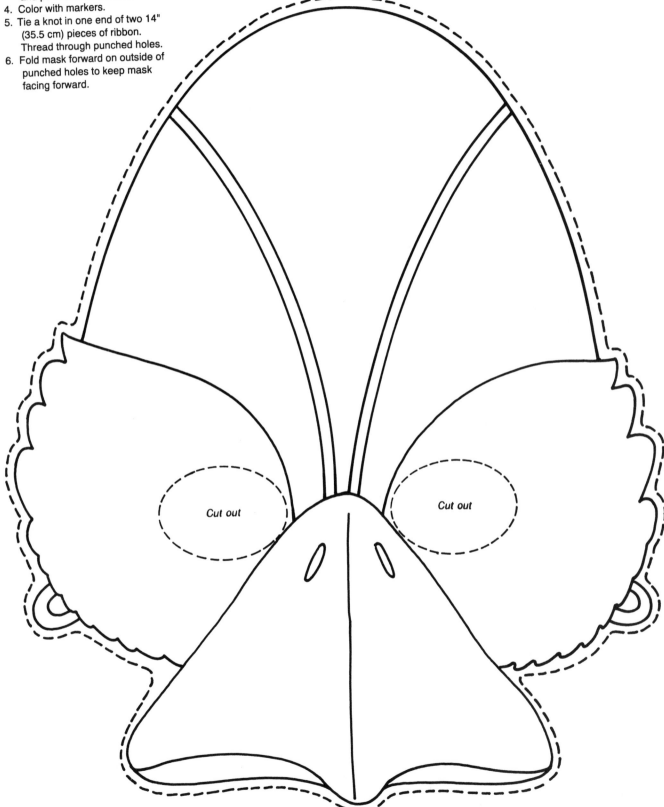

Cut out

Cut out

How to Do Plays with Children

Cow Mask

1. Reproduce mask on card stock.
2. Cut mask on dotted lines.
3. Cut eye holes with Exacto knife and punch holes for ribbon.
4. Color with markers.
5. Tie a knot in one end of two 14" (35.5 cm) pieces of ribbon. Thread through punched holes.
6. Fold mask forward on outside of punched holes to keep mask facing forward.

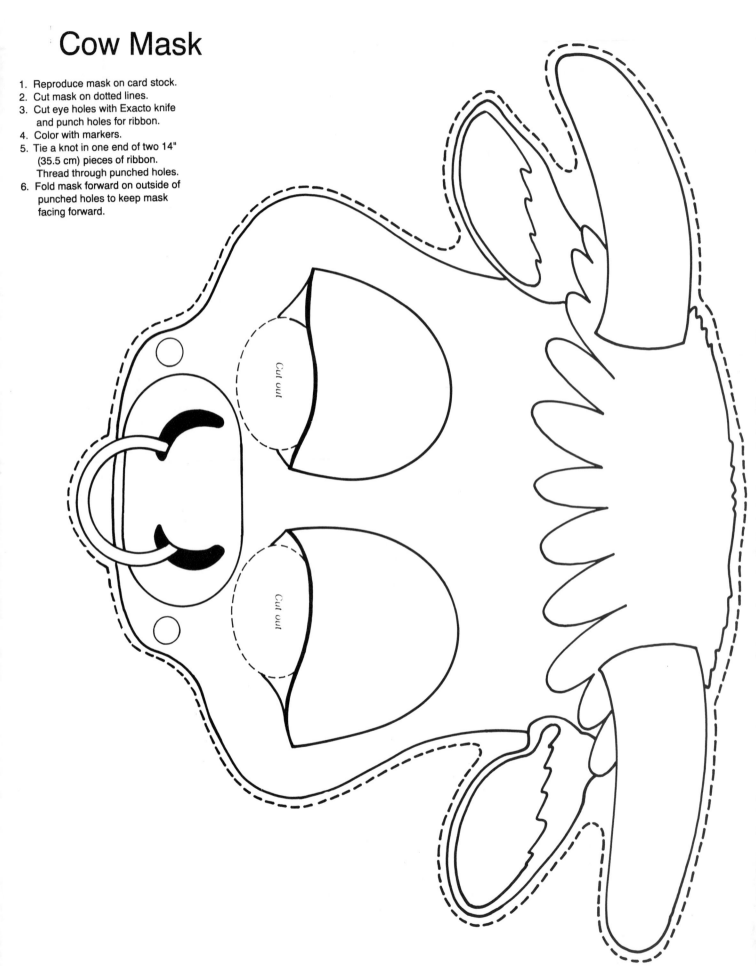

Cut out

Cut out

How to Do Plays with Children

Pig Mask

1. Reproduce mask on card stock.
2. Cut mask on dotted lines.
3. Cut eye holes with Exacto knife and punch holes for ribbon.
4. Color with markers.
5. Tie a knot in one end of two 14" (35.5 cm) pieces of ribbon. Thread through punched holes.
6. Fold mask forward on outside of punched holes to keep mask facing forward.

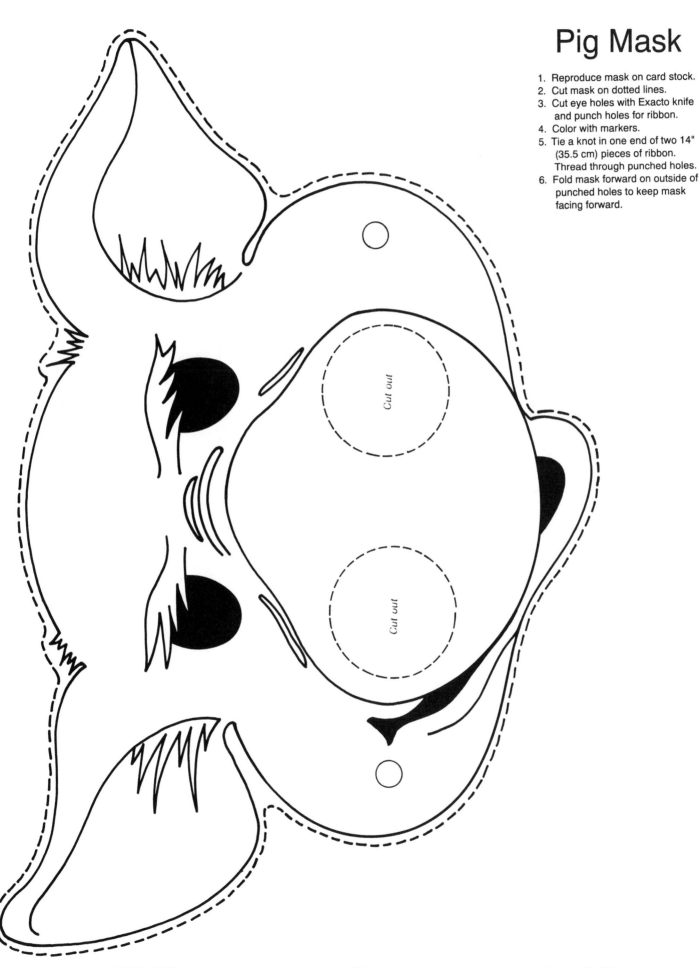

Cut out

Cut out

How to Do Plays with Children

Sheep Mask

1. Reproduce mask on card stock.
2. Cut mask on dotted lines.
3. Cut eye holes with Exacto knife and punch holes for ribbon.
4. Color with markers.
5. Tie a knot in one end of two 14" (35.5 cm) pieces of ribbon. Thread through punched holes.
6. Fold mask forward on outside of punched holes to keep mask facing forward.

How to Do Plays with Children

Rabbit Mask

Cut out

Cut out

1. Reproduce mask on card stock.
2. Cut mask on dotted lines.
3. Cut eye holes with Exacto knife and punch holes for ribbon.
4. Color with markers.
5. Tie a knot in one end of two 14" (35.5 cm) pieces of ribbon. Thread through punched holes.
6. Fold mask forward on outside of punched holes to keep mask facing forward.

How to Do Plays with Children

Match

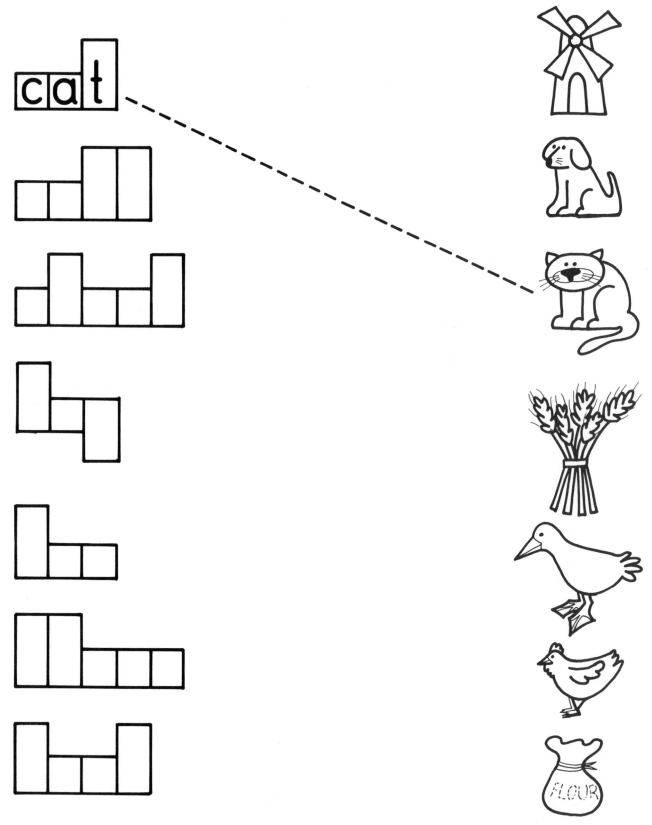

cat **wheat** **hen** **duck**

mill **dog** **lamb** **flour**

How to Do Plays with Children

The Little Red Hen
Script

**Barnyard
Chorus - Cows,
Sheep, Pigs, and
Rabbits**

Let us set the scene for you.
By the pond there stands a mill,
And down the road a barnyard
Where things are quiet and still.

The dog, the cat, and the duck
Are having a lovely day.
Now all three have stopped to listen.
Red Hen has something to say.

*Chorus recites from
their position on stage.
They will remain in
this position
throughout the play.*

Red Hen:

Look! I've found a grain of wheat.
Just think of what I could do.
I'll dig a hole and plant it.
I just need some help from you.

*Red Hen stands in
the center of the
stage, bends down,
and picks up an
imaginary grain of
wheat. She walks over
to the dog as she says
her lines.*

Dog:

Sorry, but I can't help you.
Why don't you go ask the cat?
I need to chase my ball now,
So out of my way—please scat.

*Dog is playing with his
ball. Direct the child
not to bounce the ball
or let it roll away from
him. When Dog
finishes his lines, Red
Hen walks over
to cat.*

Cat:

I'm over due for my cat nap.
Why don't you go ask the duck?
I need my nine a.m. rest.
Now go—goodbye and good luck.

*Cat is in the sleeping
position. She looks
at Red Hen as she
says her lines. Seeing
Cat won't help, Red
Hen walks back to the
center just as the
Duck passes by.*

         How to Do Plays with Children

Duck:

Help you dig a hole you ask?
This time I'll have to say no.
I'm ready for a nice swim,
So off to the millpond I go.

Duck "waddles" across the stage. He pauses next to the Red Hen long enough to say his lines and then waddles back toward the pond.

Barnyard Chorus - Cows:

They all refused to help.
They all refused to help.
She did it by herself.
She did it with no help.

Sung to the tune of "The Farmer In The Dell."

As the chorus says their lines, Red Hen puts on her garden gloves and plants her imaginary seed. Be sure she pushes some dirt over it. As the chorus finishes their lines, Red Hen stands up the stalk of wheat prop that is already in position on the floor next to her.

Red Hen:

Now it's time to cut the wheat.
Just think of what I could do.
I'll go get something to cut with.
I just need some help from you.

She looks at the stalk of wheat and then walks over to Dog.

Dog:

Sorry, but I can't help you.
Why don't you go ask the cat?
I need to chase my stick now,
So out of my way—please scat.

Dog's props should be lined up beside him so he can simply pick them up as needed. His props are: ball, stick, and sock.

Red Hen walks to cat.

Cat changes to another sleeping position.

Cat:

I'm overdue for my catnap.
Why don't you go ask the duck?
I need my twelve o'clock rest.
Now go—goodbye and good luck.

Red Hen walks back to her center position as Duck approaches.

Duck:

Help you cut the wheat you ask?
This time I'll have to say no.
I'm ready for a nice swim,
So off to the millpond I go.

Duck's directions are are the same as before.

Barnyard Chorus - Sheep:

They all refused to help.
They all refused to help.
She did it by herself.
She did it with no help.

Sung to the tune of "The Farmer In The Dell."

Red Hen:

Now it's time to thresh the wheat.
Just think of what I could do.
I'll beat the stalks with my flail.
I just need some help from you.

Red Hen pretends to cut wheat. She picks up her flail prop and the stalks of wheat. She walks over to the dog carrying the stalks and the flail.

Dog:

Sorry, but I can't help you.
Why don't you go ask the cat?
I need to chase my sock now.
So out of my way—please scat.

Dog picks up the sock and begins playing with it. Red Hen walks on to Cat.

Cat:

I'm overdue for my catnap.
Why don't you go ask the duck?
I need my two p.m. rest.
Now go—goodbye and good luck.

Cat changes to another sleeping position.

Duck:

Help you thresh the wheat you ask?
This time I'll have to say no.
I'm ready for a nice swim,
So off to the millpond I go.

Red Hen walks back to her center position as Duck approaches.

Duck waddles up to Red Hen, says his lines, and waddles back to the millpond.

Barnyard Chorus - Pigs:

Sung to the tune of "The Farmer In The Dell."

> They all refused to help.
> They all refused to help.
> She did it by herself.
> She did it with no help.

Red Hen flails her wheat here.

Red Hen:

> I'll take the grain to the mill.
> Just think of what they will do.
> They'll grind it into flour.
> Who'll help me carry it—will you?

Red Hen gets brown bag from behind table. She walks over to the dog carrying the brown pillowcase prop.

Dog:

Dog chases his tail.

> Sorry, but I can't help you.
> Why don't you go ask the cat?
> I need to chase my tail now,
> So out of my way—please scat.

Cat changes to another sleeping position.

Cat:

> I'm overdue for my catnap.
> Why don't you go ask the duck?
> I need my four p.m. rest.
> Now go—goodbye and good luck.

Red Hen walks back to the center of the stage as Duck approaches.

Duck waddles up to Red Hen, says his lines, and waddles back to the pond.

Duck:

> Help you take it to the mill?
> This time I'll have to say no.
> I'm ready for a nice swim,
> So off to the millpond I go.

Red Hen carries the brown sack to the mill. She walks behind the mill and picks up the white sack marked "flour."

Barnyard Chorus - Rabbits:

They all refused to help.
They all refused to help.
She did it by herself.
She did it with no help.

Sung to the tune of "The Farmer In The Dell."

Red Hen carries the sack of flour into her house and puts on her apron while the barnyard chorus is singing.

Red Hen:

Now it's time to make some bread.
Just think of what I could do.
I'll knead the dough—then bake it.
I just need some help from you.

Red Hen says her lines from behind her window, speaking through the window.

Dog:

Sorry, but I can't help you.
Why don't you go ask the cat?
I need to chase my ball now,
So out of my way—please scat.

Dog is playing with his ball. Direct the child not to bounce the ball or let it roll away from him. When Dog finishes his lines, Red Hen walks over to cat.

Cat:

I'm overdue for my catnap.
Why don't you go ask the duck?
I need my five p.m. rest.
I say no, but I still wish you luck.

Cat assumes the sleeping position.

Duck:

Make flour into bread you ask?
This time I'll have to say no.
I'm ready for a nice swim,
So off to the millpond I go.

Duck waddles over to Red Hen's window, says his lines, and then waddles to the pond.

Barnyard Chorus - All:

They all refused to help.
They all refused to help.
She did it by herself.
She did it with no help.

Sung to the tune of "The Farmer In The Dell."

Suddenly the dog stopped chasing.
The cat rubbed her sleepy eyes.
The duck waddled up from the pond.
They all smelled a great surprise.

Duck, Dog, and Cat all rush to Red Hen's window just as she is setting the fresh baked bread on the windowsill. The animals kneel down outside her window and say their lines.

Dog:

Oh, how I love home-made bread.

Cat:

I'm hungry from resting all day.

Duck:

I want a piece from the end.

Red Hen:

Wait! I have something to say.

You wouldn't help plant the grain,
Cut or carry the wheat.
I did it all by myself,
And now you expect to eat?

 How to Do Plays with Children

Red Hen:

I plan to eat this bread myself.
Next time maybe you'll learn
That sometimes the things we want,
We have to work for and earn.

When Red Hen finishes her last line she actually eats a pre-cut piece of bread. The dog, cat, and duck turn to face the audience and sit Indian style. They rest their chins on their hands and look very sad.

Barnyard Chorus - All:

They all refused to help.
They all refused to help.
She ate it all herself.
She did it with no help.

How to Do Plays with Children

Lines one and three change in the first five stanzas.

Red Hen:

Look! I've found a grain of wheat
Just think of what I could do.
I'll dig a hole and plant it.
I just need some help from you.

Now it's time to cut the wheat.
Just think of what I could do.
I'll go get something to cut with.
I just need some help from you.

Now it's time to thresh the wheat.
Just think of what I could do.
I'll beat the stalks with my flail.
I just need some help from you.

I'll take the grain to the mill.
Just think of what they will do.
They'll grind it into flour.
Who'll help me carry it - will you?

Now it's time to make some bread.
Just think of what I could do.
I'll knead the flour - then bake it.
I just need some help from you.

Wait! I have something to say.

You wouldn't help plant the grain,
Cut or carry the wheat.
I did it all by myself,
And now you expect to eat?

I plan to eat this bread myself.
Next time maybe you'll learn
That sometimes the things we want,
We have to work for and earn.

Take-Home Practice Script

Dear Parent - Please help your child learn these lines for a class play. Thank you.

Line three changes in each stanza.

Dog:

Sorry, but I can't help you.
Why don't you go ask the cat?
I need to chase my ball now,
So out of my way - please scat.

Sorry, but I can't help you.
Why don't you go ask the cat?
I need to chase my stick now,
So out of my way - please scat.

Sorry, but I can't help you.
Why don't you go ask the cat?
I need to chase my sock now.
So out of my way - please scat.

Sorry, but I can't help you.
Why don't you go ask the cat?
I need to chase my tail now,
So out of my way - please scat.

Sorry, but I can't help you.
Why don't you go ask the cat?
I need to chase my ball now,
So out of my way - please scat.

Oh, how I love home-made bread.

Line one changes in each stanza.

Duck:

Help you dig a hole you ask?
This time I'll have to say no.
I'm ready for a nice swim,
So off to the millpond I go.

Help you cut the wheat you ask?
This time I'll have to say no.
I'm ready for a nice swim,
So off to the millpond I go.

Help you thresh the wheat you ask?
This time I'll have to say no.
I'm ready for a nice swim,
So off to the millpond I go.

Help you take it to the mill?
This time I'll have to say no.
I'm ready for a nice swim,
So off to the millpond I go.

Make flour into bread you ask?
This time I'll have to say no.
I'm ready for a nice swim,
So off to the millpond I go.

I want a piece from the end.

Take-Home Practice Script
Dear Parent - Please help your child learn
these lines for a class play. Thank you.

Line three changes in each stanza.

Cat:

I'm overdue for my cat nap.
Why don't you go ask the duck?
I need my nine a.m. rest.
Now go - goodbye and good luck.

I'm overdue for my catnap.
Why don't you go ask the duck?
I need my twelve o'clock rest.
Now go - goodbye and good luck.

I'm overdue for my catnap.
Why don't you go ask the duck?
I need my two p.m. rest.
Now go - goodbye and good luck.

I'm overdue for my catnap.
Why don't you go ask the duck?
I need my four p.m. rest.
Now go - goodbye and good luck.

I'm overdue for my catnap.
Why don't you go ask the duck?
I need my five p.m. rest.
I say no, but I still wish you luck.

I'm hungry from resting all day.

**Barnyard
Chorus - Cows,
Sheep, Pigs, and
Rabbits.**

Sung to the tune of
The Farmer In The Dell

Let us set the scene for you.
By the pond there stands a mill,
And down the road a barnyard
Where things are quiet and still.

The dog, the cat, and the duck
Are having a lovely day.
Now all three have stopped to listen.
Red Hen has something to say.

Suddenly the dog stopped chasing.
The cat rubbed her sleepy eyes.
The duck waddled up from the pond.
They all smelled a great surprise.

They all refused to help.
They all refused to help.
She did it by herself.
She did it with no help.

They all refused to help.
They all refused to help
She ate it all herself.
She did it with no help.

class:

presents the play

The Little Red Hen

date:

time:

place:

Please join us!

 How to Do Plays with Children

The Little Red Hen

Red Hen: _____

Dog: _____

Cat: _____

Duck: _____

Barnyard Chorus -

Cows: Pigs:

Sheep: Rabbits:

Goldilocks
and
the Three Bears
by Leslie Tryon

Scenery 109

Characters and Costumes.......... 111

Props 112

Masks 113

Hidden Picture Activity 116

Script 117

Take-Home Practice Script 126

Invitation 132

Play Program............................. 133

Scenery

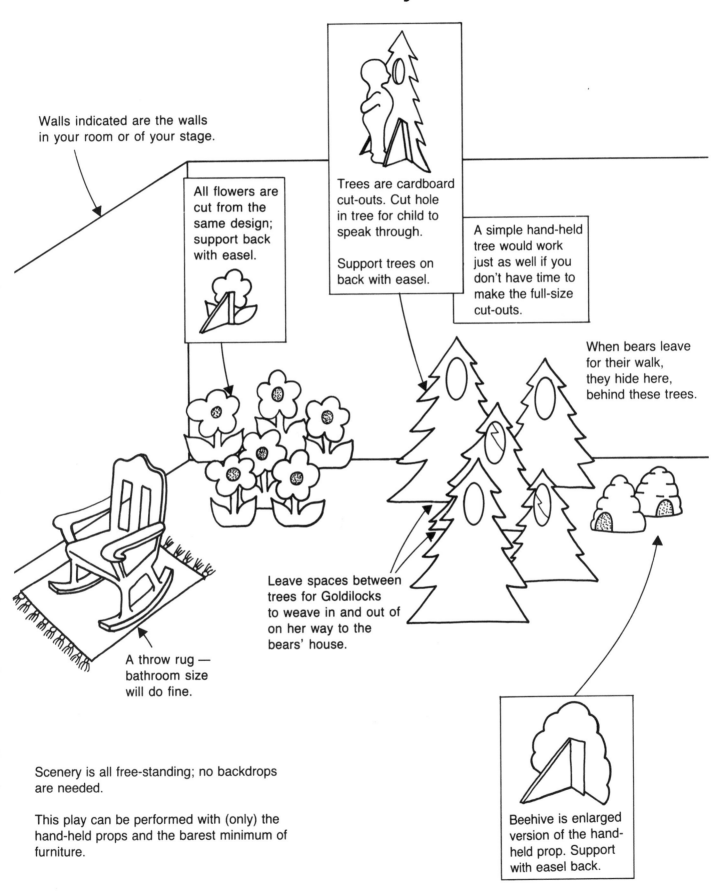

Walls indicated are the walls in your room or of your stage.

All flowers are cut from the same design; support back with easel.

Trees are cardboard cut-outs. Cut hole in tree for child to speak through.

Support trees on back with easel.

A simple hand-held tree would work just as well if you don't have time to make the full-size cut-outs.

When bears leave for their walk, they hide here, behind these trees.

A throw rug — bathroom size will do fine.

Leave spaces between trees for Goldilocks to weave in and out of on her way to the bears' house.

Beehive is enlarged version of the hand-held prop. Support with easel back.

Scenery is all free-standing; no backdrops are needed.

This play can be performed with (only) the hand-held props and the barest minimum of furniture.

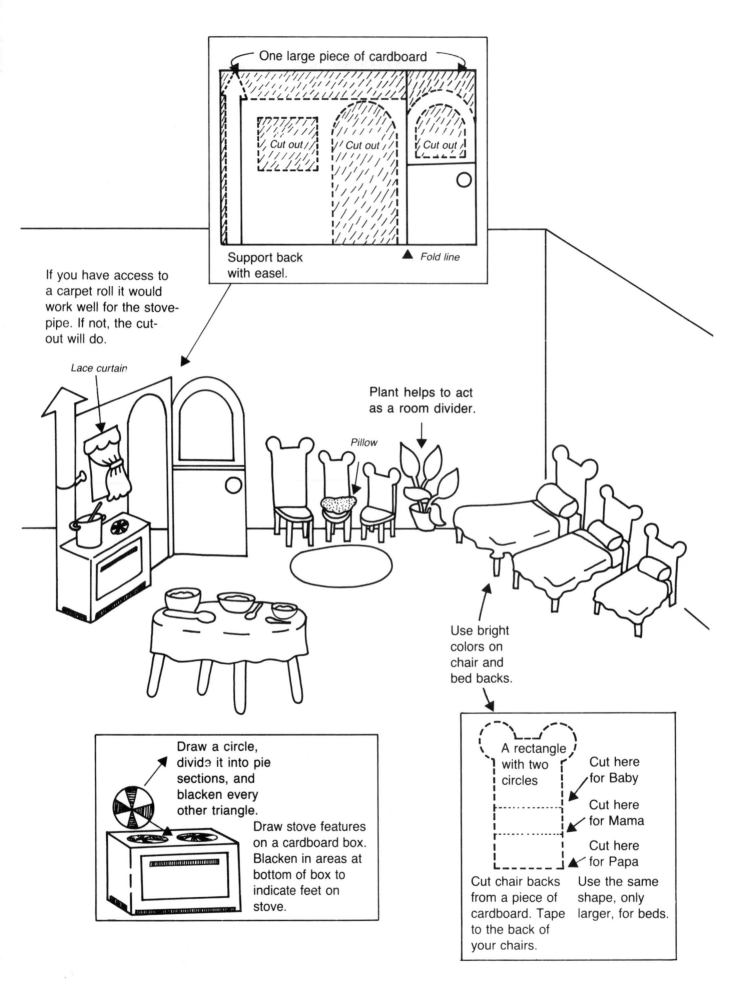

One large piece of cardboard

Cut out

Cut out

Cut out

Support back with easel.

▲ Fold line

If you have access to a carpet roll it would work well for the stove-pipe. If not, the cut-out will do.

Lace curtain

Plant helps to act as a room divider.

Pillow

Use bright colors on chair and bed backs.

Draw a circle, divide it into pie sections, and blacken every other triangle.

Draw stove features on a cardboard box. Blacken in areas at bottom of box to indicate feet on stove.

A rectangle with two circles

Cut here for Baby

Cut here for Mama

Cut here for Papa

Cut chair backs from a piece of cardboard. Tape to the back of your chairs.

Use the same shape, only larger, for beds.

How to Do Plays with Children

Characters and Costumes

Tree chorus wears running suits or school clothes. If you choose to use the hand-held props, ask your students to wear dark colors.

Goldilocks chorus wears dark pants and skirts, and white, or light, shirts.

The bees wear clothes appropriate for sitting on the floor. We recommend a running suit.

The headband is made by attaching pipe cleaners to a sweatband.

The flower wears clothes appropriate for sitting on the floor.

Mama Bear wears a running suit, an apron, and carries the bear mask.

Papa Bear wears a running suit, a man's tie, and carries the bear mask.

Baby Bear wears a running suit and carries a teddy bear and the bear mask.

Have all three bears wear the same color suits if at all possible.

Goldilocks wears purple socks and a VERY LARGE red bow.

The easiest solution for the gold hair is to have a blonde child take the part.

If you need to fashion the hair, use yarn or construction paper.

Construction paper is the simplest. Cut the paper in narrow strips, leaving an inch at the top. Make several rows of this paper fringe. Roll each strip on a pencil to create a curl. Staple to a headband and cover top with bow.

Mother wears an apron and glasses. She could be reading, knitting, or peeling apples.

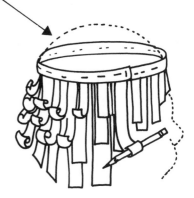

How to Do Plays with Children

Props

Three bowls

Three spoons

A soup pot

Ladle

Three pillows

Three blankets

Tablecloth

Two throw rugs

Hand-Held Props

Flower

Beehive

Bear mask

Furniture

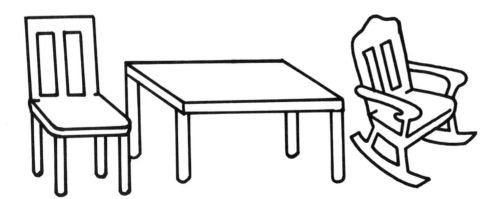
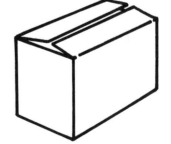

Three chairs

Three tables for beds

Rocker
(if available)

Cardboard box
for stove

How to Do Plays with Children

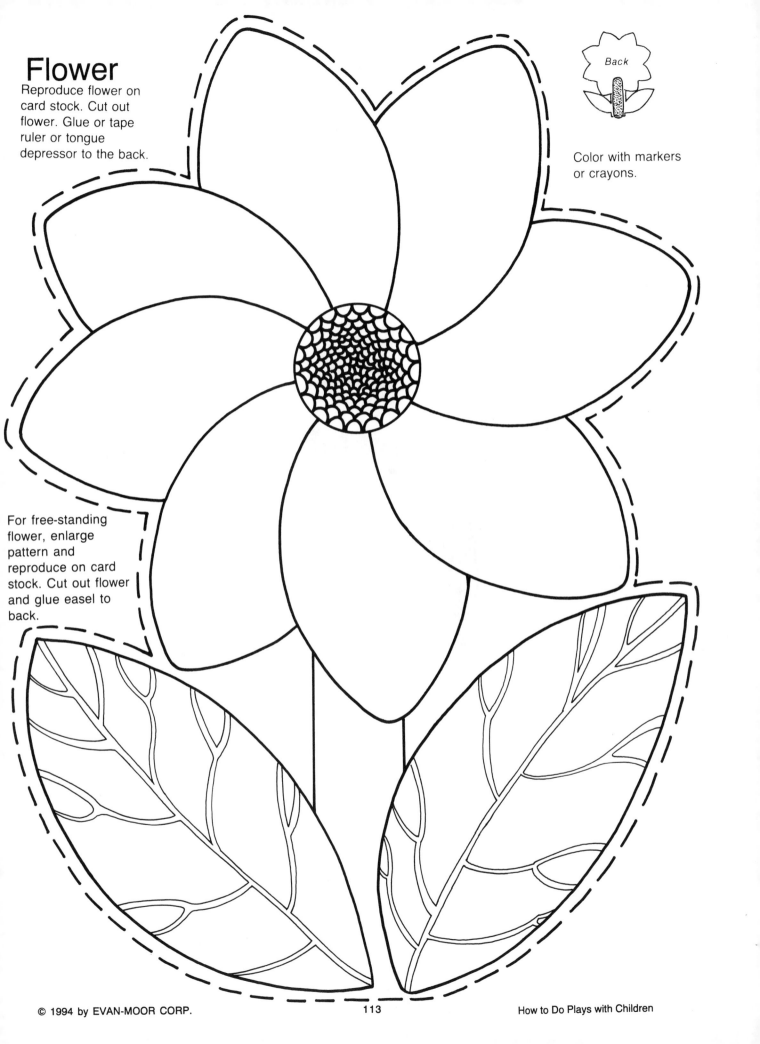

Flower

Reproduce flower on card stock. Cut out flower. Glue or tape ruler or tongue depressor to the back.

Back

Color with markers or crayons.

For free-standing flower, enlarge pattern and reproduce on card stock. Cut out flower and glue easel to back.

How to Do Plays with Children

Bear Mask
Happy

Reproduce mask in 3 different sizes: big for Papa Bear, middle size for Mama Bear and smaller for Baby Bear.

Reproduce mask on card stock. Cut out mask. Glue or tape ruler or tongue depressor to the back. Glue grumpy and

happy masks back-to-back with the tongue depressor between. Color with markers or crayons.

Back

How to Do Plays with Children

Bear Mask
Grumpy

Reproduce mask on card stock. Cut out mask.

Color with markers or crayons.

Back

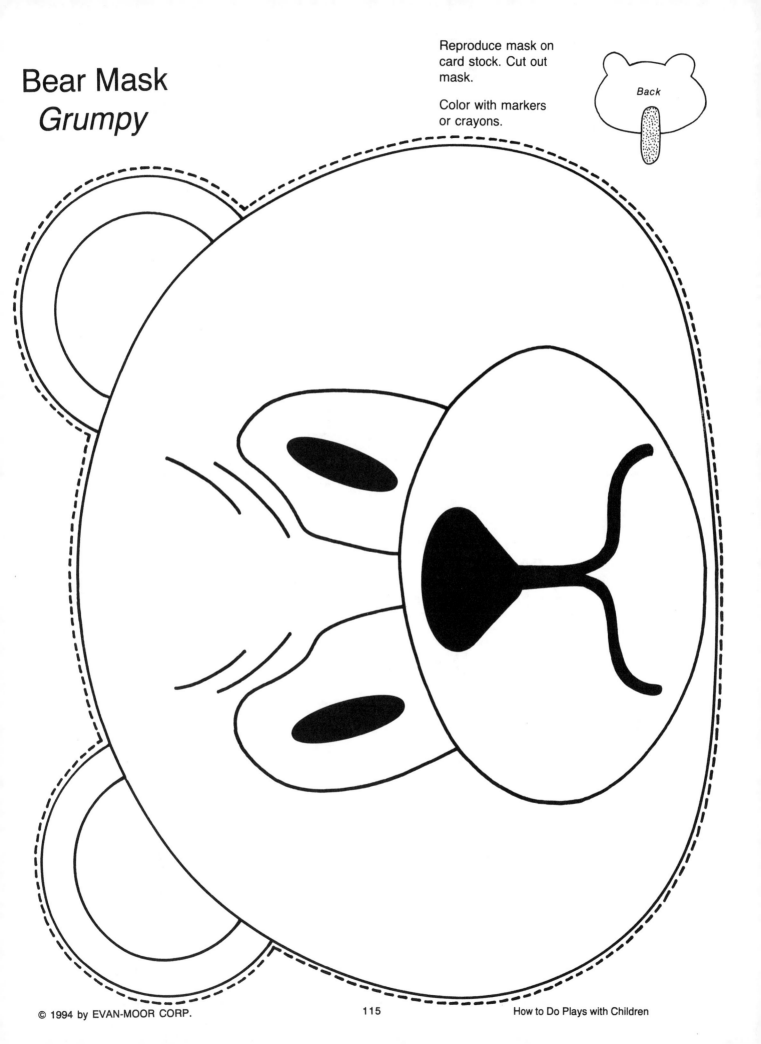

How to Do Plays with Children

HIDDEN PICTURE

116

How to Do Plays with Children

Goldilocks and the Three Bears
Script

Goldilocks
Chorus:

Goldilocks
Wore purple socks,
And a big red bow
In her hair.

She knew a dog,
A cat, and a frog;
But had never
Met a bear.

Goldilocks enters stage right and walks over to her mother's chair.

Mother:

I'll tie your bow,
Then out you go.
Stay close to the house
And play.

Be a good girl, please.
Don't go near the trees,
Or in your room
You'll stay.

Mother says her lines while sitting in her chair. Direct her to rock ONLY when she says her lines. She remains in the chair for the rest of the play.

Flower:

Goldilocks is here!
Oh dear! Oh dear! Oh dear!
That bad girl
With the golden hair.

She stomps and skips,
Twirls and trips,
Till our blossoms
And petals are bare.

One flower child is on his or her knees in the flower patch holding flower prop. On last two lines "till our blossoms and petals are bare" child switches to stick with leaves only.

Goldilocks
Chorus:

Goldilocks
Wore purple socks,
And a big red bow
In her hair.

She knew a dog,
a cat, and a frog,
But had never
Met a bear.

*Goldilocks romps and
stomps her way through
the flowers as the
chorus repeats the
refrain.*

Tree
Chorus:

Meanwhile...

Deep in the trees,
By the pond, where the bees
Hide away
From the bears living there,

In a warm little place
With curtains of lace,
Live Papa, and Mama,
And little Baby Bear

*Goldilocks walks into
the forest and hides
behind one tree until
the bears leave.*

Mama
Bear:

The porridge is hot
If it stays in the pot,
So into the bowls
It goes.

It can cool while we talk
And go for a walk.
But right now it's too hot —
Heaven knows.

*Papa Bear and Baby
Bear are sitting in their
chairs.
Mama Bear tests the
porridge as she repeats
her lines.
Mama Bear fills the
three bowls and takes
them to the table.
The bears go the table
and discover the bowls.*

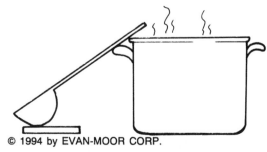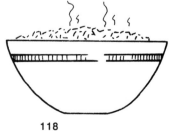

How to Do Plays with Children

**Tree
Chorus:**

Deep in the trees
By the pond, where the bees
Hide away
From the bears living there,

In a warm little place
With curtains of lace,
Live Papa, and Mama,
And little Baby Bear.

*The three bears
leave their house
and go into the
forest. Bears hide
behind the trees.*

**Goldilocks
Chorus:**

That bad little girl
With the golden curl
Disobeyed her mother;
She did.

She went deep in the trees
To the pond where the bees
Said "Go back!"
Then quickly they hid.

*Goldilocks weaves her
way through the trees
to the house.
Bees watch her
wide-eyed;
then hide their faces
behind their beehives.*

She went into the place
With the curtains of lace.
She didn't even knock
Or say please.

The table was set
With the porridge, and yet
There was no one around
But those bees.

*Goldilocks enters the
house of the three bears
and goes to the table.*

Bee
Chorus:

With no time to waste,
She took a quick taste
From the big bowl
And cried, "It's too hot!"

The next one she tried
Made her all cold inside,
And she turned up her nose
On the spot.

*Goldilocks can join in
with the bees on
"...It's too hot!"*

Goldilocks:

My grumbly tummy
Wants something real yummy,
So I'll try this last bowl
And see.

*Goldilocks "eats" the
bowl of porridge.*

I'll just take a bite —
Hooray — it's just right!
It must have been left
Just for me.

How to Do Plays with Children

Chair #1:

Now that her tummy
Has had something yummy,
She looked for a place
To sit down.

A chair with a seat
Not so high that her feet
Dangle up in the air
Off the ground.

My seat is hard
Like the dirt in the yard,
So I'll thank you to
Sit over there.

Each chair has a child sitting in it. Papa Bear's chair holds his arms over his head and when he says "Sit over there," he brings his arm down and points to the next chair.

Goldilocks goes from one chair to the next as the chairs say their lines.

Chair #2:

My seat is as soft
As the hay in the loft,
It's not right for you
So beware.

Goldilocks:

This one's just right,
But I think if I might
Find a bed
I've a minute to spare.

Stretching and yawning, she sits in Baby Bear's chair.

Chair #3:

Please get off my lap,
And go take your nap
On a bed that you'll find
Over there.

Goldilocks gets up clumsily and "breaks" chair # 3. Chair # 3 points to the beds as he says his last line and pretends to be broken.

How to Do Plays with Children

Goldilocks:

This one's too hard
Like the dirt in the yard,
Not at all a nice place
For a rest.

This one's too soft
Like the hay in the loft.
I'll bet that the
Small one is best.

*Goldilocks goes from
one bed to the next as
she says her lines.*

**Bee
Chorus:**

The small one was best,
So she took a nice rest.
Before long she lay
Counting sheep.

She heard not a sound
When those bears came around.
She was tucked in the bed
Fast asleep.

*Goldilocks lies down on
Baby Bear's bed and
goes to sleep.*

*Bears return from their
walk.*

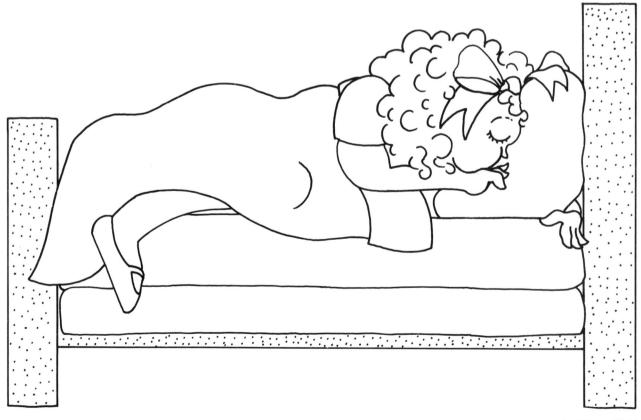

Papa Bear:

My spoon's in my bowl!
Look out! Heads will roll!
Someone's been eating
My porridge!

*The bears go to the table
and discover the bowls.
Each bear says his lines
standing behind his bowl.*

*Each bear switches
to the grumpy mask
as they say their lines.*

Mama Bear:

Mine's all wrong too!
Whatever will I do?
Someone's been eating
My porridge!

Baby Bear:

I think that I'll cry
Cause mine's gone bye-bye!
Someone's been here
And they ate all my porridge!

Papa Bear:

Hold onto your hat!
If it wasn't the cat,
Then someone's been
Sitting in my chair.

*The bears discover the
chairs next. Direct bears
to sit in the chairs as
they say their lines.*

Mama Bear:

I just can't believe it!
I may have a snit fit!
Someone's been
Sitting in my chair.

Baby Bear:

Well I'm hopping mad!
Someone's really been bad!
They've sat here
And broken my chair.

Tree Chorus:

Papa Bear, Mama Bear,
And little Baby Bear,
In a rage to the bedroom
They sped.

Papa Bear cried,
And Mama Bear sighed,
Someone's been sleeping
Right here in my bed.

Bee Chorus:

We all looked about
When we heard a loud shout.
From that tiny one
Little Baby Bear.

Baby Bear:

Right here in my bed,
Is a big bow of red,
And a girl underneath
With gold hair.

**Bee
Chorus:**

Goldilocks' eyes
Opened up with surprise.
She tried, but her legs
Wouldn't go.

*Goldilocks awakes and
sees the three bears
standing over the bed.*

**Three
Bears:**

Get out of that bed
While you still have a head,
Or we'll eat you —
Right up to your bow!

**Tree
Chorus:**

She ran past the bees,
The pond and the trees,
Past the flowers
As fast as she could.

*Goldilocks runs out of
the house and weaves
her way through the
trees and the flowers
back to her mother.*

Her mother was mad
Because she was bad,
But she gave her a
Hug. It felt good.

**Goldilocks
Chorus:**

Goldilocks
Wore purple socks,
And a big red bow
In her hair.

She knew a dog,
A cat, and a frog,
And now she
Knew three bears.

   How to Do Plays with Children

Bee Chorus:

With no time to waste,
She took a quick taste
From the big bowl
And cried, "It's too hot!"

The next one she tried
Made her all cold inside,
And she turned up her nose
On the spot.

The small one was best,
So she took a nice rest.
Before long she lay
Counting sheep.

She heard not a sound
When those bears came around.
She was tucked in the bed
Fast asleep.

We all looked about
When we heard a loud shout
From that tiny one
Little Baby Bear.

Goldilocks' eyes
Opened up with surprise.
She tried, but her legs
Wouldn't go.

Goldilocks:

My grumbly tummy
Wants something real yummy,
So I'll try this last bowl
And see.

I'll just take a bite -
Hooray - it's just right!
It must have been left
Just for me.

This one's just right,
But I think if I might
Find a bed
I've a minute to spare.

This one's too hard
Like the dirt in the yard,
Not at all a nice place
For a rest.

This one's too soft
Like the hay in the loft.
I'll bet that the
Small one is best.

Take-Home Practice Script
Dear Parent - Please help your child learn
these lines for a class play. Thank you.

Mother:

I"ll tie your bow,
Then out you go.
Stay close to the house
And play.

Be a good girl, please.
Don't go near the trees,
Or in your room
you'll stay.

Take-Home Practice Script
Dear Parent - Please help your child learn
these lines for a class play. Thank you.

Papa Bear:

My spoon's in my bowl!
Look out! Heads will roll!
Someone's been eating
My porridge!

Hold onto your hat!
If it wasn't the cat,
Then someone's been
Sitting in my chair.

Three Bears:

Get out of that bed
While you still have a head,
Or we'll eat you -
Right up to your bow!

Take-Home Practice Script
Dear Parent - Please help your child learn
these lines for a class play. Thank you.

Chair #2:

My seat is as soft
As the hay in the loft,
It's not right for you
So beware.

Take-Home Practice Script
Dear Parent - Please help your child learn
these lines for a class play. Thank you.

Chair #3:

Please get off my lap,
And go take your nap
On a bed that you'll find
Over there.

Take-Home Practice Script
Dear Parent - Please help your child learn
these lines for a class play. Thank you.

Goldilocks Chorus:

Goldilocks
Wore purple socks,
And a big red bow
In her hair.

She knew a dog,
A cat, and a frog,
But had never
Met a bear.

That bad little girl
With the golden curl
Disobeyed her mother;
She did.

She went deep in the trees
To the pond where the bees
Said "Go back!"
Then quickly they hid.

She went into the place
With the curtains of lace.
She didn't even knock
Or say please.

The table was set
With the porridge, and yet
There was no one around
But those bees.

Goldilocks
Wore purple socks,
And a big red bow
in her hair.

She knew a dog,
A cat, and a frog,
And now she
Knew three bears.

Mama Bear:

The porridge is hot
If it stays in the pot,
So into the bowls
It goes.

It can cool while we talk
And go for a walk.
But right now it's too hot -
Heaven knows.

Mine's all wrong too!
Whatever will I do?
Someone's been eating
My porridge!

I just can't believe it!
I may have a snit fit!
Someone's been
Sitting in my chair.

Three Bears:

Get out of that bed
While you still have a head,
Or we'll eat you -
Right up to your bow!

Flower:

Goldilocks is here!
Oh dear! Oh dear! Oh dear!
That bad girl
With the golden hair.

She stomps and skips,
Twirls and trips,
Till our blossoms
and petals are bare.

Tree Chorus:

Meanwhile...

Deep in the trees,
By the pond, where the bees
Hide away
From the bears living there,

In a warm little place
With curtains of lace,
Live Papa, and Mama,
And little Baby Bear

Deep in the trees
By the pond, where the bees
Hide away
From the bears living there,

In a warm little place
With curtains of lace,
Live Papa, and Mama,
And Little Baby Bear

Papa Bear, Mama Bear,
And little Baby Bear,
In a rage to the bedroom
They sped.

Papa Bear cried,
And Mama Bear sighed,
Someone's been sleeping
Right here in my bed.

She ran past the bees,
The pond and the trees,
Past the flowers
As fast as she could.

Her mother was mad
Because she was bad,
But she gave her a hug.
It felt good.

Baby Bear:

I think that I'll cry
Cause mine's gone bye-bye!
Someone's been here
And they ate all my porridge!

Well I'm hopping mad!
Someone's really been bad!
They've sat here
And broken my chair.

Right here in my bed,
Is a big bow of red,
And a girl underneath
With gold hair.

Three Bears:

Get out of that bed
While you still have a head,
Or we'll eat you -
Right up to your bow!

Chair #1:

Now that her tummy
Has had something yummy,
She looked for a place
To sit down.

A chair with a seat
Not so high that her feet
Dangle up in the air
Off the ground.

My seat is hard
Like the dirt in the yard,
So I'll thank you to
Sit over there.

class:

presents the play

Goldilocks and the Three Bears

date:

time:

place:

Please join us!

How to Do Plays with Children

Goldilocks and the Three Bears

Goldilocks: _____

Mama Bear: _____

Papa Bear: _____

Baby Bear: _____

Mother: _____

Flower: _____

Chair #1: _____

Chair #2: _____

Chair #3: _____

Bee Chorus:

Tree Chorus:

Goldilocks
Chorus:

A Flea on Santa's Tree?

by Leslie Tryon

Scenery 135

Characters and Costumes......... 136

Masks 137

Props 145

Word Search Activity 146

Script 147

Take-Home Practice Script 154

Invitation 157

Play Program........................... 158

How to Do Plays with Children

Scenery

The only scenery required is a cut-out Christmas tree. A small step-stool placed behind the tree makes a place for the children to stand as they recite.

Cut out top of tree for child's head to rest on. When a child stands behind the tree, all the viewer should see is his/her head.

Santa needs a nice big chair to sit in.

How to Do Plays with Children

Characters and Costumes

The guardian angel wears a white blouse and skirt, shoes and socks. Running shoes or tennis shoes will do. She wears an apron, and a watch. See diagram for wings. Make halo from pipe cleaners. Tape "GA" to blouse.

Elves wear short, calf-length pants; bright socks and T-shirts. Tie a bright scarf around their waist or a wide ribbon if they don't have a scarf.

Cut two triangles of felt for each elf hat. Glue or sew together.   Turn up edge to form cuff and glue pom-pom to the point. Each elf can wear a different color hat.

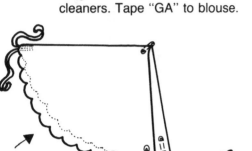

Make two.
Any light fabric will do.
Pin at shoulder and waist.

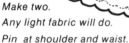

Children who wear masks should wear dark clothes.

Masks - pages 138-144.

You will need a Santa suit, or anything red you can stuff and add a cotton beard to.

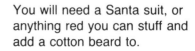

Masked Characters

1. Reproduce and color the masks on the following pages.
   Special instructions are included with each mask.

2. The masks are designed to be attached to construction paper strips to create the bands that go around the students' heads. Fit each headband to the individual students' head.

3. Characters who wear masks should wear a dark shirt and pants.

1. Reproduce mask on card stock.
2. Cut mask on dotted lines.
3. Cut eye holes with Exacto knife and punch holes for ribbon.
4. Color with markers.
5. Tie a knot in one end of two 14" (35.5 cm) pieces of ribbon. Thread through punched holes.
6. Fold mask forward on outside of punched holes to keep mask facing forward.

Owl

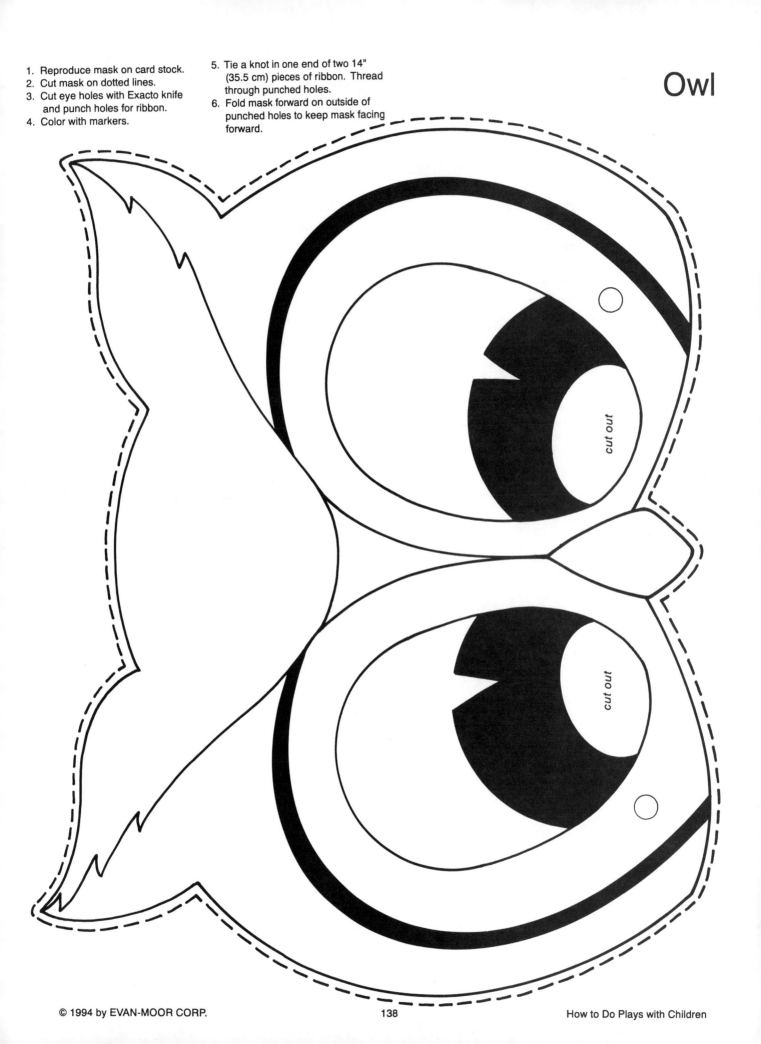

cut out

cut out

How to Do Plays with Children

Queen's Crown

1. Reproduce crown on card stock twice and cut out.
2. Staple or tape two of the ends together.
3. Color with markers.
4. Fit to child's head and staple or tape the remaining ends together.

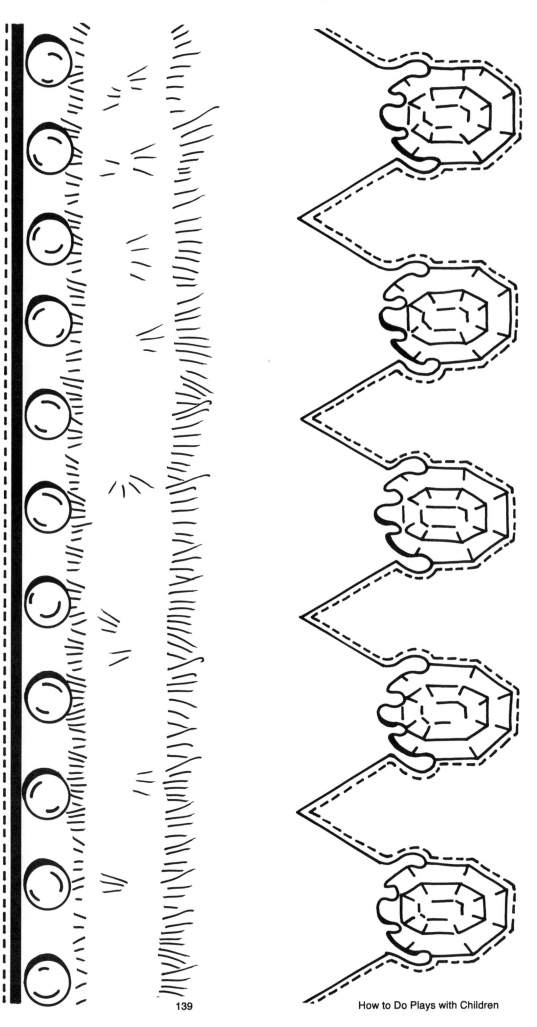

How to Do Plays with Children

Apple

1. Reproduce mask on card stock.
2. Cut mask on dotted lines.
3. Cut eye holes with Exacto knife and punch holes for ribbon.
4. Color with markers.
5. Tie a knot in one end of two 14" (35.5 cm) pieces of ribbon. Thread through punched holes.
6. Fold mask forward on outside of punched holes to keep mask facing forward.

cut out

cut out

How to Do Plays with Children

Flower

cut out

cut out

1. Reproduce mask on card stock.
2. Cut mask on dotted lines.
3. Cut eye holes with Exacto knife and punch holes for ribbon.
4. Color with markers.
5. Tie a knot in one end of two 14" (35.5 cm) pieces of ribbon. Thread through punched holes.
6. Fold mask forward on outside of punched holes to keep mask facing forward.

How to Do Plays with Children

Elephant

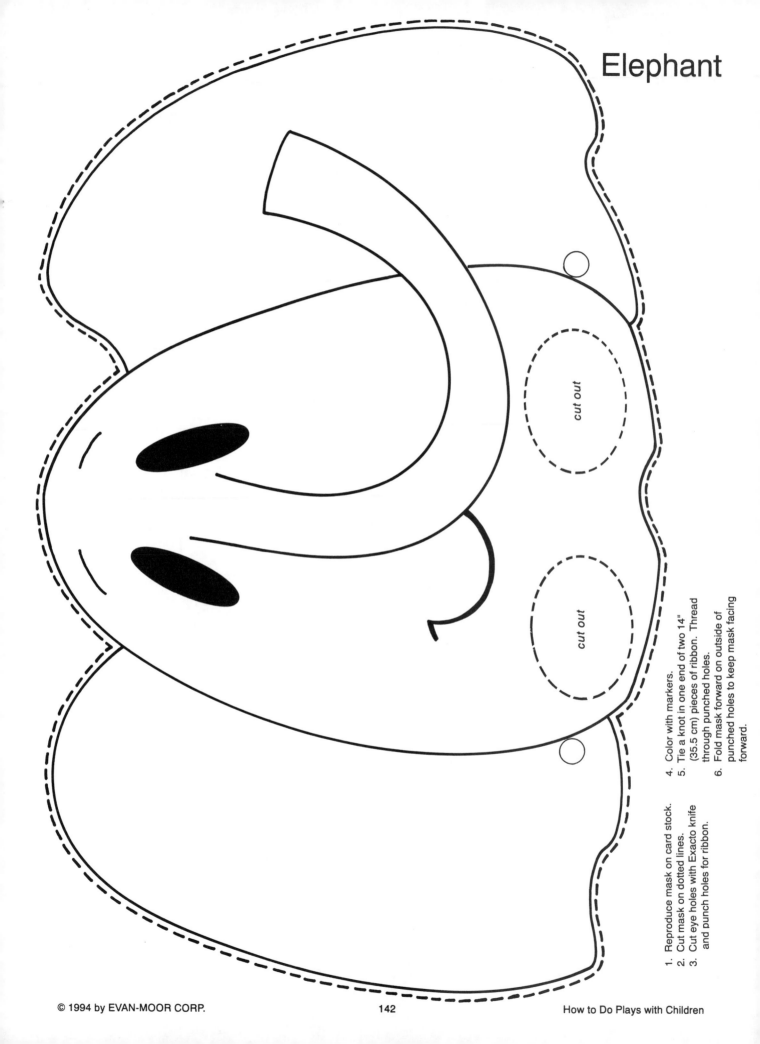

cut out

cut out

1. Reproduce mask on card stock.
2. Cut mask on dotted lines.
3. Cut eye holes with Exacto knife and punch holes for ribbon.
4. Color with markers.
5. Tie a knot in one end of two 14" (35.5 cm) pieces of ribbon. Thread through punched holes.
6. Fold mask forward on outside of punched holes to keep mask facing forward.

How to Do Plays with Children

Flea

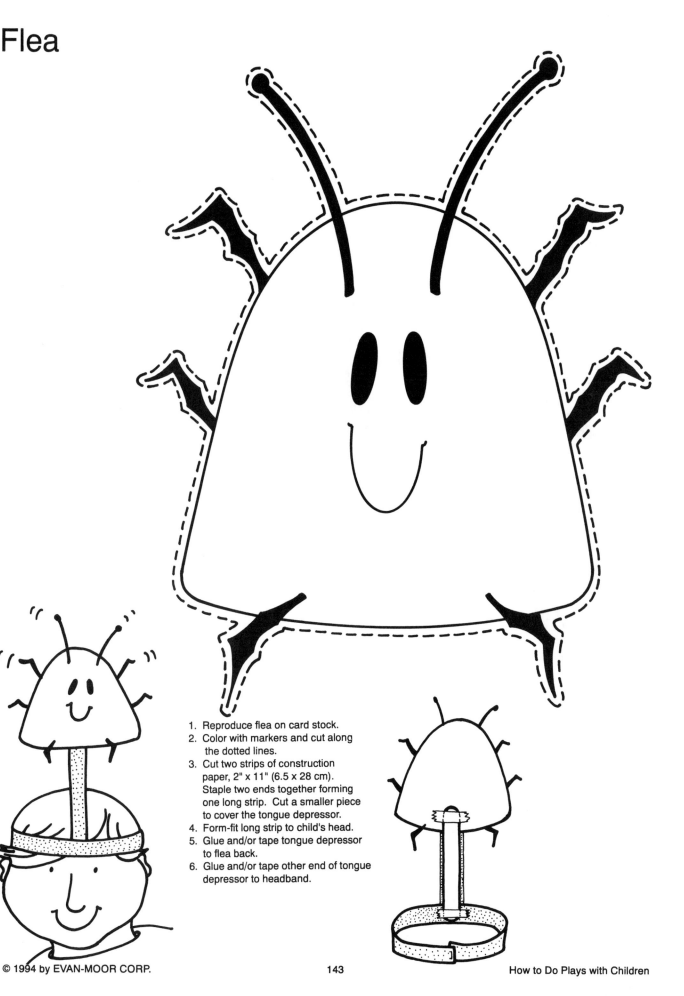

1. Reproduce flea on card stock.
2. Color with markers and cut along the dotted lines.
3. Cut two strips of construction paper, 2" x 11" (6.5 x 28 cm). Staple two ends together forming one long strip. Cut a smaller piece to cover the tongue depressor.
4. Form-fit long strip to child's head.
5. Glue and/or tape tongue depressor to flea back.
6. Glue and/or tape other end of tongue depressor to headband.

How to Do Plays with Children

Martian

Color Martian green.

cut out

cut out

Glue or staple pipe cleaners here.

1. Reproduce mask on card stock.
2. Cut mask on dotted lines.
3. Cut eye holes with Exacto knife and punch holes for ribbon.
4. Color with markers.

5. Tie a knot in one end of two 14" (35.5 cm) pieces of ribbon. Thread through punched holes.
6. Fold mask forward on outside of punched holes to keep mask facing forward.

How to Do Plays with Children

Props

Reproduce ornaments on card stock, several copies each. Color with markers.
This would make a good activity for your students.

145 How to Do Plays with Children

Word Search

f l e a n p l a y m
a n f l o w e r b e
t e l e p h a n t l
q u e e n w e o r v
o s a n t a i w e e
m a r t i a n l e s
a p p l e a n g e l

angel		flea	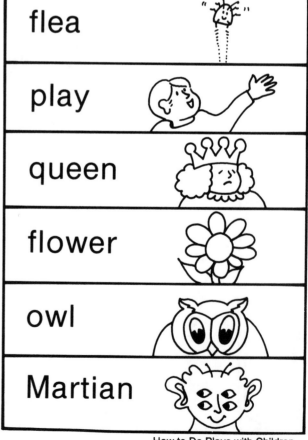
apple		play	
elephant		queen	
elves		flower	
Santa		owl	
tree		Martian	

How to Do Plays with Children

A Flea on Santa's Tree?
Script

Elves:

'Tis Christmas Eve
And Santa's tree
Is naked at the top.

He did his best
To make it nice
But then he had to stop.

Santa:

It isn't right
The top is bare
It needs a special thing.

Send out a call
Throughout the land
To all ears listening.

Santa points to tree, then directs his lines to the audience.

Elves:

Now is your chance
A try for fame
A chance to be the top.

And when we've found
The very best
We'll bring this to a stop.

Chorus addresses its lines to the audience. The characters to audition come from the back of the room as though they have come from the audience.

Elephant:

Just give me nuts
And lots of room
To balance way up high.

I'll hold my breath
I'll think real thin
If you'll just let me try.

Elves:

Thank you but no
You're not quite right
For now you just won't do.

There's more in line
So please step down
Don't call us—we'll call you.

Elf chorus looks at Santa. Santa shakes his head no, the chorus then says their lines.

Children will exit to side.

Flea:

Please let me stay
Atop your tree
I'm not in search of fame.

I only want
To be the one
To give fleas a good name.

Elf chorus looks at Santa. He shakes his head no, the chorus then says their lines.

Elves:

Thank you but no
You're not quite right
For now you just won't do.

There's more in line
So please step down
Don't call us—we'll call you.

The flea shakes his antenna and hops off

Santa's guardian angel:

Please Santa dear
It is my job
To take good care of you.

So take a break
And eat some lunch
Because it's good for you.

The angel enters wearing an apron and drying her hands on a towel as though she has just come from the kitchen. She could also be wearing a pot holder mitt.

Santa:

Not now — not now
Please can't it wait?
You see I just can't stop.

It's Christmas Eve
And still it's bare
My poor tree has no top.

Santa waves her away, not really even looking at her.

The angel exits, aggravated.

Queen:

Just step aside
You motley lot
This treetop is for me

A queen will get
Just what she wants
As you will plainly see.

*The queen is **very** unlikable. She holds her nose high in the air.*

The queen exits.

Elves:

Thank you but no
You're not quite right
For now you just won't do.

There's more in line
So please step down
Don't call us-we'll call you.

The angel enters and looks at Santa. He shakes his head no and waves her away. She exits, hands on hips. very aggravated.

Flower:

I've had my fill
Of flower pots
So please give me a try.

Just don't say no
'Cause if you do
I'll break right down and cry.

The flower does her lines like a spoiled child.

Elf chorus looks at Santa. Santa says no, etc.

Elves:

Thank you but no
You're not quite right
For now you just won't do,

There's more in line
So please step down
Don't call us—we'll call you.

The flower exits crying.

The angel enters, looks at Santa, and points to her watch. Santa shakes his head no. She stomps her foot and storms off.

Martian:

An outer space face
All nice and green
I came here from the stars.

Just think, your tree
Could be the first
To boast a top from Mars.

Elf chorus looks at Santa. Santa nods no, etc.

Elves:

Thank you but no
You're not quite right
For now you just won't do.

There's more in line
So please step down
Don't call us—we'll call you.

Martian bobs his feelers and makes a Martian-like exit. (Whatever that is.)

150   How to Do Plays with Children

The angel enters, arms folded, looking very mad. Santa says no again and waves her away. She stomps her little angel foot and storms off stage.

Apple:

My friends have all
Wound up in pies
Or jars — that's not for me.

I'll rise above
That common place
To star-here on your tree.

Elves:

Thank you but no
You're not quite right
For now you just won't do.

There's more in line
So please step down
Don't call us-we'll call you.

Elf chorus looks at Santa. He says no, etc.

The apple says ''Well!'' And exits in a huff.

The angel enters, hands on her hips and presses her nose right up to his. Santa just raises one hand and points for her to exit. She jumps up and down, then storms off.

How to Do Plays with Children

Owl:

This treetop work
Is just my style
I'd say it's my strong suit.

Make me your choice
It would be wise
To show you give a hoot.

Elf chorus looks at Santa. Santa nods no, etc.

Elves:

Thank you but no
You're not quite right
For now you just won't do.

There's more in line
So please step down
Don't call us–we'll call you.

Owl:

Well! Whooooo do you think you are?

The owl says his additional line and exits.

The angel has had it. She decides the only way she is going to get Santa's attention is to speak to him from atop the tree.

Guardian Angel:

I've waved my wings
I've stomped my foot
And now your lunch is cold.

And still you sit
Wrapped up in work
It's time for me to scold.

She says her lines while waving her wings; she is mad.

As she says her lines Santa moves foreward in his seat as he realizes he has found his perfect tree-topper.

Santa: You're perfect, stop —
        Don't move a hair
        Quick — tell her she's just right.

Santa holds his hand up and gestures for her to stay; he looks very happy.

His last line is directed to the elf chorus.

Elves: Thank you, you'll do
        In fact you're great!
        A really lovely sight.

Elf chorus   'Tis Christmas Eve
and all who   And Santa's tree
tried out: Looks great- and now you know.

        That's how the angel
        Got up there
        So now you all can go.

               How to Do Plays with Children

Elves:

'Tis Christmas Eve
And Santa's tree
Is naked at the top.

He did his best
To make it nice
But then he had to stop.

Now is your chance
A try for fame
A chance to be the top.

And when we've found
The very best
We'll bring this to a stop.

Thank you but no
You're not quite right
For now you just won't do.

There's more in line
So please step down
Don't call us - we'll call you.

Thank you, you'll do
In fact you're great!
A really lovely sight.

'Tis Christmas Eve
And Santa's tree
Looks great and now you know.

That's how the angel
Got up there
So now you all can go.

- -

Santa:

It isn't right
The top is bare
It needs a special thing.

Send out a call
Throughout the land
To all ears listening.

Not now - not now.
Please can't it wait?
You see I just can't stop.

It's Christmas Eve
And still it's bare;
My poor tree has no top.

You're perfect, stop -
Don't move a hair
Quick - tell her she's just right.

Owl:

This treetop work
Is just my style
I'd say it's my strong suit.

Make me your choice
It would be wise
To show you give a hoot.

Well! Whoooooo do you
think you are?

Guardian Angel:

Please Santa dear
It is my job
To take good care of you.

So take a break
And eat some lunch
Because it's good for you.

I've waved my wings
I've stomped my foot
And now your lunch is cold.

And still you sit
Wrapped up in work.
It's time for me to scold.

Apple:

My friends have all
Wound up in pies
Or jars - that's not for me.

I'll rise above
That common place
To star here on your tree.

Flea:

Please let me stay
Atop your tree
I'm not in search of fame.

I only want
To be the one
To give fleas a good name.

Martian:

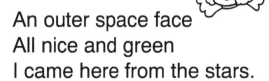

An outer space face
All nice and green
I came here from the stars.

Just think your tree
Could be the first
To boast a top from Mars.

Flower:

I've had my fill
Of flower pots
So please give me a try.

Just don't say no
'Cause if you do
I'll break right down and cry.

- -

Queen:

Just step aside
You motley lot
This treetop is for me

A queen will get
Just what she wants
As you will plainly see.

- -

Elephant:

Just give me nuts
And lots of room
To balance way up high.

I'll hold my breath
I'll think real thin
If you'll just let me try.

class:

presents the play

A Flea on Santa's Tree?

date:

time:

place:

Please join us!

A Flea on Santa's Tree?

Santa: _____

Elephant: _____

Flea: _____

Guardian Angel: _____

Queen: _____

Flower: _____

Martian: _____

Apple: _____

Owl: _____

Elves: _____

   How to Do Plays with Children

A Rhyming Play
Fun for Everyone

Spring Starts Here!
by Leslie Tryon

Scenery 160

Characters and Costumes 161

Masks 162

Raindrops 168

Props 169

Script 173

Take-Home Practice Script 180

Invitation 185

Play Program 186

How to Do Plays with Children

Scenery

Cut irregular cloud shapes out of butcher paper. Tape clouds to existing light fixtures or punch holes and hang them from the ceiling.

Use tables to support raindrops. Any arrangement will do as long as they are all gathered under the clouds at different levels. Rain and clouds are behind Weather Station.

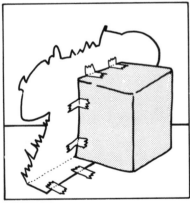

Cut a half-circle in one side of a large cardboard box.

Use this drawing as a pattern. Project onto butcher paper. The pattern for the Weather Station sign is on page 171.

Tape butcher paper cut-out to box. Cut a matching hole in the paper using the box as a guide.

Fold back part of butcher paper cut-out and tape to floor.

See page 179 for final arrangement of characters on stage.

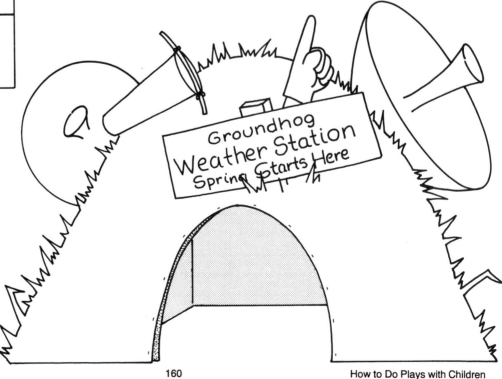

Groundhog
Weather Station
Spring Starts Here

Characters and Costumes

Rabbit

Rabbit wears his ears and large glasses. Whiskers are drawn on. An all-white running suit is worn with white socks on his hands and feet. Rabbit is grumpy and pushy.

Spring Chicken

Spring Chicken wears his or her mask. Spring Chicken is a baby with a baby-like voice. This character can wear a big bow if a girl or a baseball cap if a boy. Costume is a yellow running suit worn with orange socks on feet.

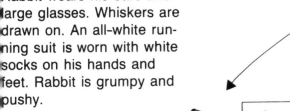

Raindrops

This is the chorus, the more the merrier. Raindrops (see diagram) are worn on chest, and at the last minute open up to reveal the spring flowers. Costumes should be light or white clothes of any type.

Butterfly

Butterfly wears her mask. She "flutters" whenever she is onstage. She wears tights and a plain T-shirt (black or brown). See diagram on page 165 for wings and feelers.

Max

Max wears his mask. The costume should be dark brown, perhaps a running suit worn with black socks on his hands and feet.

■ All characters, except the raindrops, carry the rainbow/umbrella (See page 170.)

■ Narrator wears a lightly colored running suit. Add a scarf, hat and mittens to emphasize the weather condition.

Robin

Robin wears her mask. Robin has the motherly look, a little old hat, glasses and a big red bow with streamers hanging down her chest. A pale-colored running suit is worn with yellow socks on her feet.

Pig

Pig wears his or her mask. Pig should be portly. Stuff the costume if necessary. Pig wears a pink running suit with brown socks on hands and feet. Pig prop is a box filled with fake food props (see illustration).

Robin

1. Reproduce mask on card stock.
2. Cut on dotted lines.
3. Cut eye holes with Exacto knife and punch holes for ribbon.
4. Color with markers.
5. Tie a knot in one end of two 14" (35.5 cm) pieces of ribbon. Thread through punched holes.
6. Fold mask forward on outside of punched holes to keep mask facing forward.

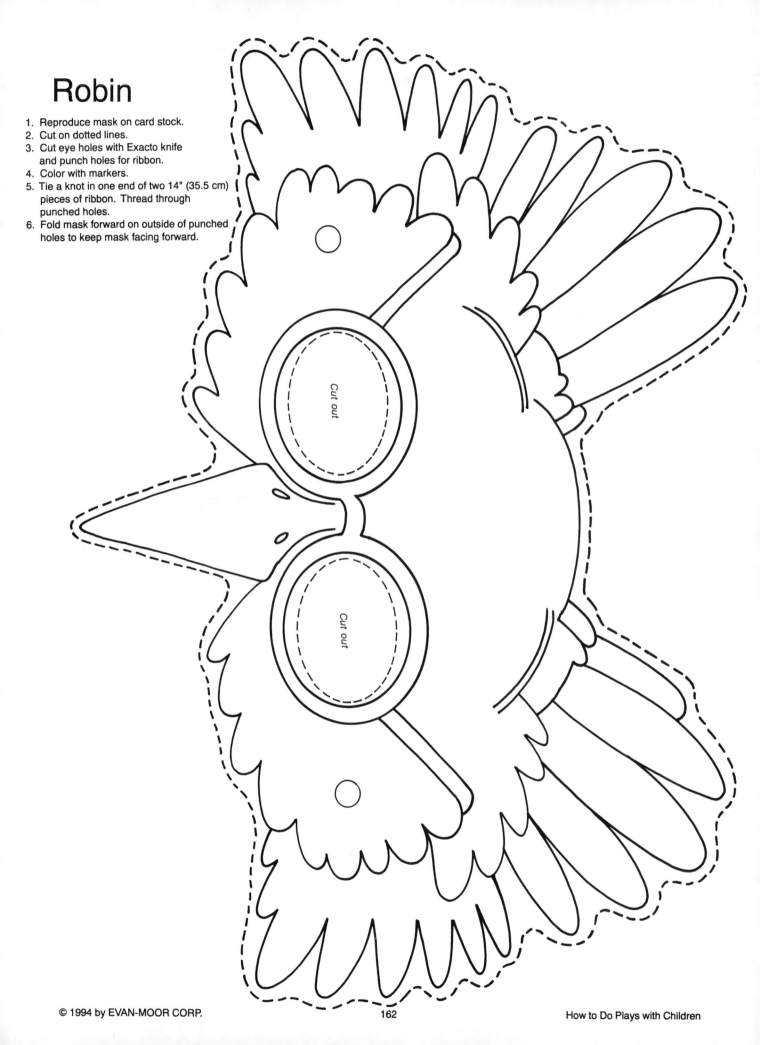

Cut out

Cut out

How to Do Plays with Children

Rabbit

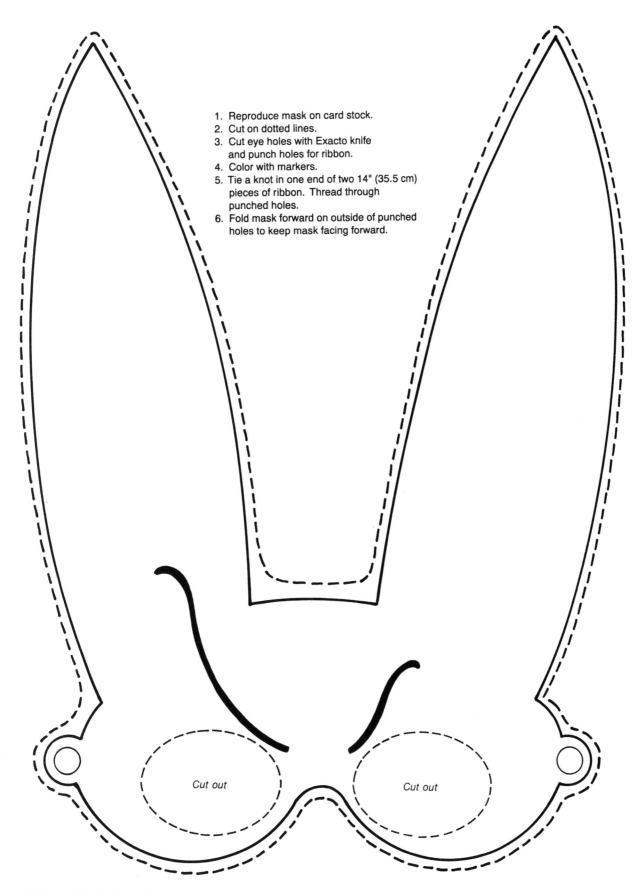

1. Reproduce mask on card stock.
2. Cut on dotted lines.
3. Cut eye holes with Exacto knife and punch holes for ribbon.
4. Color with markers.
5. Tie a knot in one end of two 14" (35.5 cm) pieces of ribbon. Thread through punched holes.
6. Fold mask forward on outside of punched holes to keep mask facing forward.

Cut out

Cut out

How to Do Plays with Children

Max

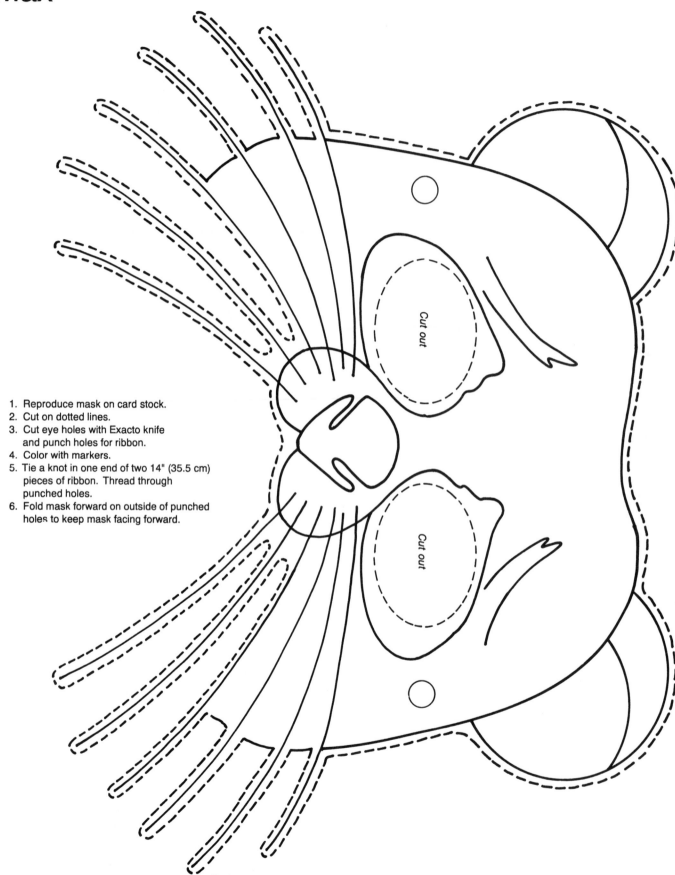

1. Reproduce mask on card stock.
2. Cut on dotted lines.
3. Cut eye holes with Exacto knife and punch holes for ribbon.
4. Color with markers.
5. Tie a knot in one end of two 14" (35.5 cm) pieces of ribbon. Thread through punched holes.
6. Fold mask forward on outside of punched holes to keep mask facing forward.

Cut out

Cut out

How to Do Plays with Children

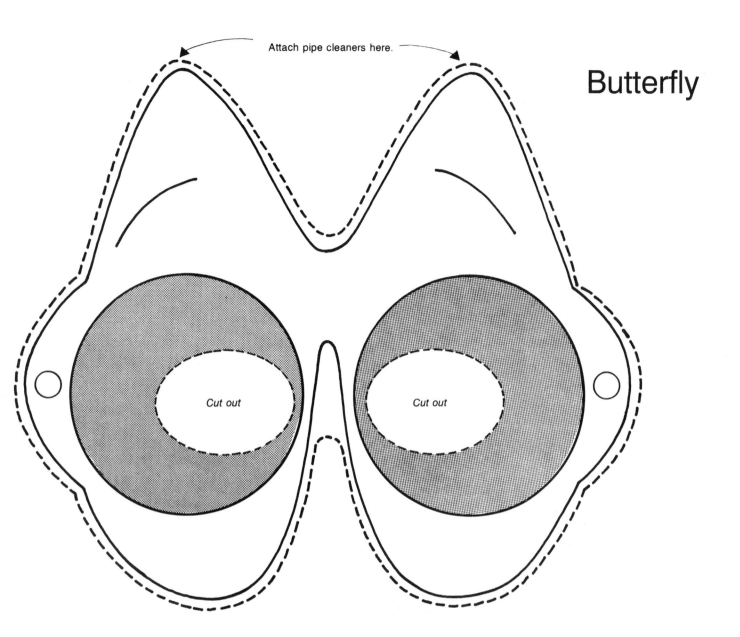

Attach pipe cleaners here.

Butterfly

Cut out

Cut out

1. Reproduce mask on card stock.
2. Cut on dotted lines.
3. Cut eye holes with Exacto knife and punch holes for ribbon.
4. Color with markers.
5. Tie a knot in one end of two 14" (35.5 cm) pieces of ribbon. Thread through punched holes.
6. Fold mask forward on outside of punched holes to keep mask facing forward.

Wings

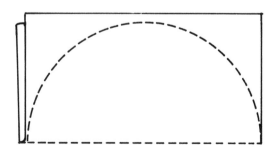

1. Cut two half-circles of any transparent and colorful fabric. You will need 40" x45" (100 x 112 cm) piece of fabric.
2. Fold half-circle in half.
3. Pin or sew a small circle of elastic at wrist. Child will slip her hand through elastic.

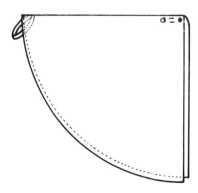

How to Do Plays with Children

Spring Chicken

1. Reproduce mask on card stock.
2. Cut on dotted lines.
3. Cut eye holes with Exacto knife and punch holes for ribbon.
4. Color with markers.
5. Tie a knot in one end of two 14" (35.5 cm) pieces of ribbon. Thread through punched holes.
6. Fold mask forward on outside of punched holes to keep mask facing forward.

Glue upper beak to mask. Fold up along dotted line to create open beak effect.

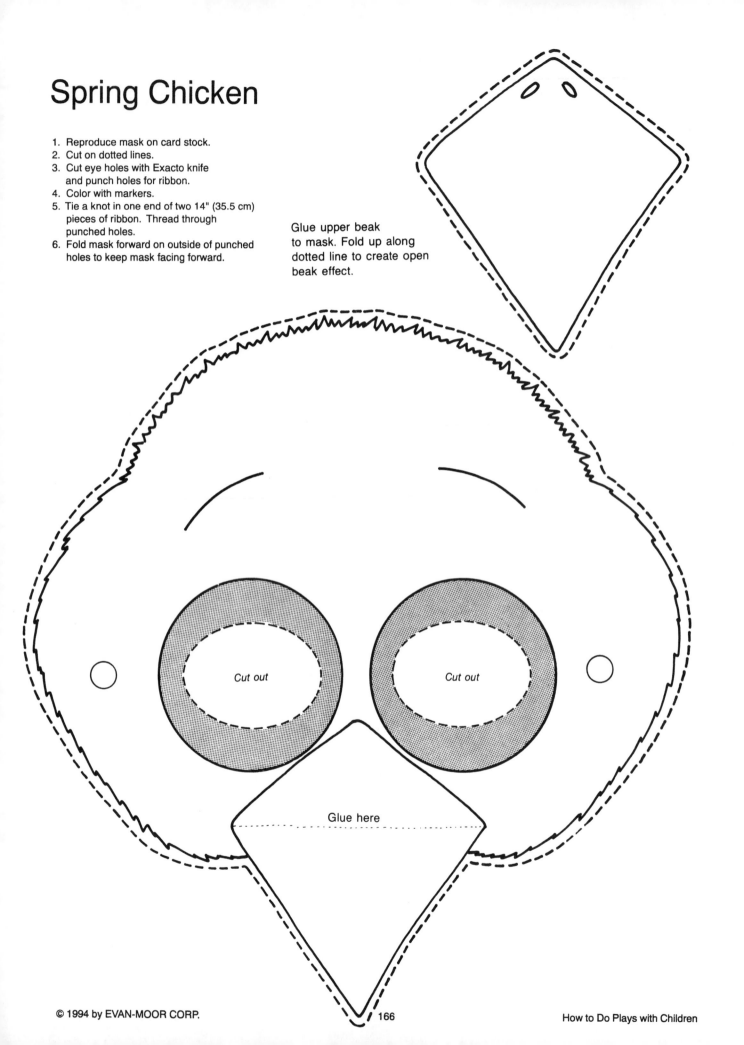

Cut out

Cut out

Glue here

How to Do Plays with Children

Pig

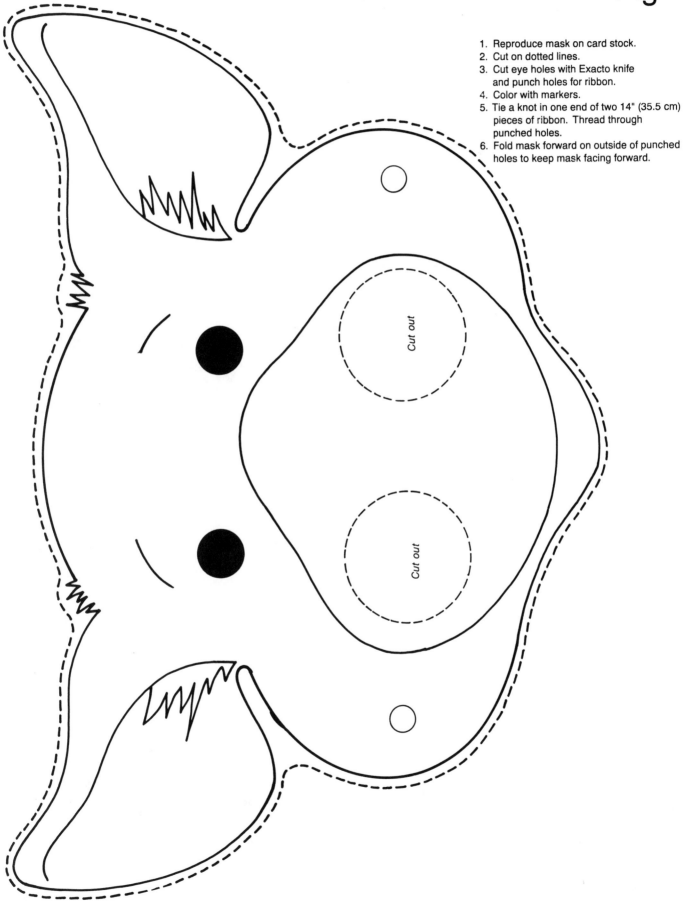

1. Reproduce mask on card stock.
2. Cut on dotted lines.
3. Cut eye holes with Exacto knife and punch holes for ribbon.
4. Color with markers.
5. Tie a knot in one end of two 14" (35.5 cm) pieces of ribbon. Thread through punched holes.
6. Fold mask forward on outside of punched holes to keep mask facing forward.

Cut out

Cut out

Raindrops

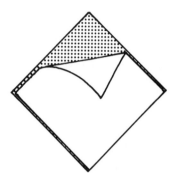

Cut two pieces of butcher paper 24" square, one white and one blue. Glue together. You can use a variety of colored papers in place of the white, if available.

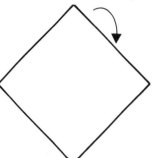

Fold in half, point-to-point.

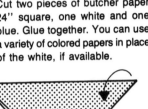

Blue side out.

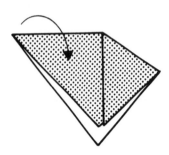

Fold one point down to meet bottom point.

Children wear raindrops until the last scene (see direction on page 178).

In the final scene they open up the raindrops themselves to reveal the flowers. If raindrops are worn too high on the chest the children will cover their faces when they open them up.

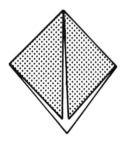

Then the other.

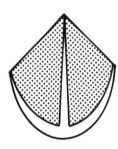

Round the points.

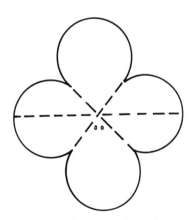

Unfold raindrop/flower. Punch two holes in bottom petal. Use a pencil.
Use markers to color flowers.

Thread yarn or roving through holes. Make the yarn long enough to slip around child's neck and have raindrop hang mid-chest.

How to Do Plays with Children

Props

Bell—Any bell will do as long as it rings.

Horn

Towel

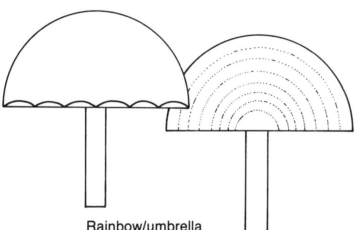

Rainbow/umbrella
(See pages 170 and 172)

Raindrop/flower
(See page 168)

Lunch sack and food props

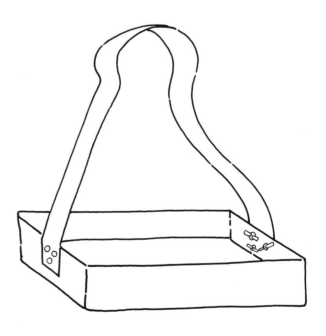

Snack box

How to Do Plays with Children

Rainbow

1. Reproduce rainbow on card stock.
2. Cut on dotted lines.
3. Color with crayons or markers. Colors are indicated on rainbow.
4. Tape ruler or stick to center back.
5. Glue umbrella to back.

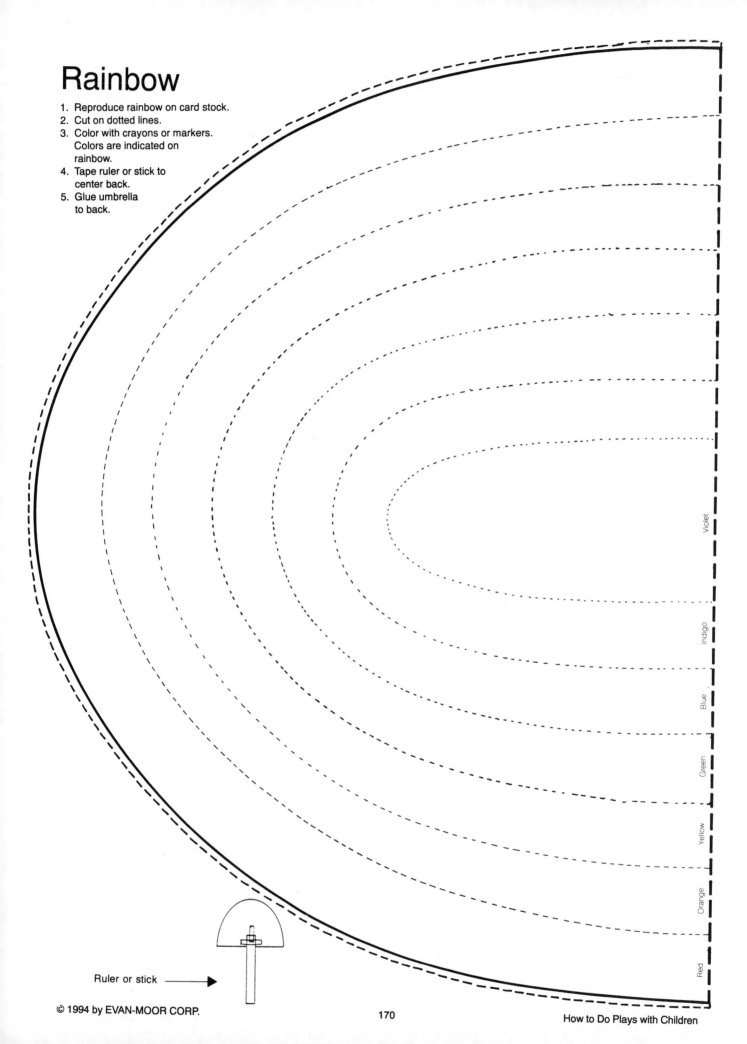

Violet

Indigo

Blue

Green

Yellow

Orange

Red

Ruler or stick ⟶

How to Do Plays with Children

Weather Station Sign

1. Reproduce sign on card stock.
2. Cut on dotted lines.
3. Color with markers.
4. Glue to weather station over the door.

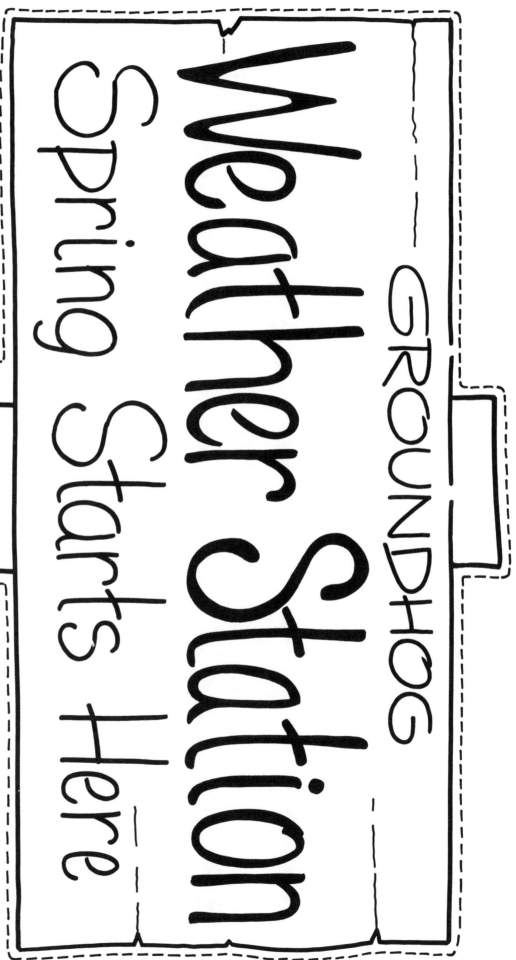

GROUNDHOG

Weather Station

Spring Starts Here

Umbrella

1. Reproduce umbrella on card stock.
2. Cut on dotted lines.
3. Color with crayons or markers.
4. Glue to rainbow back.

All characters, except the raindrops, carry the rainbow/umbrella.

How to Do Plays with Children

Spring Starts Here!
Script

Narrator:
If you feel nine stanzas are too many for one student, use two students.

The month is April.
There are clouds in the sky.
Shhh!—listen. You can hear
The rain if you try.

Max is inside his weather station, center stage. We do not see him. The narrator enters and stands to the right of the weather station. The narrator holds an umbrella, as do all the other characters.

Raindrops:

Grrr-umble, Rrrr-umble,
Zap, zap, ker-zip!
We're the April showers.
We go drip, drip, drip.

The raindrops are in place behind the weather station. The more raindrops, the merrier.

Robin:
If you feel nine stanzas are too many for one student, give one or two stanzas to another character.

There may be no spring
At all this year.
We're all still waiting
For old Max to appear.

Robin enters, walks over to the weather station, looks in, then says her lines. After she recites, she continues to look in the hole as the narrator speaks.

Narrator:

You see, Max is a groundhog
Who has the say-so,
As to the time
That winter will go.

He spends all winter long
In the ground fast asleep.
Then on February second
He comes up for a peek.

He comes out of his hole
And looks all around
To see if his shadow
Appears on the ground.

How to Do Plays with Children

Narrator:

If he sees his shadow,
Winter will stay.
If there isn't a shadow,
Then spring's on the way.

Robin:

This year we think
His alarm didn't ring.
Old Max overslept.
Now we're late for spring.

*Robin turns to face
audience and say
lines.*

*Rabbit enters as
Robin is speaking.
Rabbit looks
unhappy.*

If these showers continue
Day after day,
We'll all surely drown
And be washed away.

Rabbit:

Come out of that hole
You tired, old hog!
We'd get better service
From a lazy old dog.

*Rabbit says his lines
looking into hole.*

*Robin looks startled
at his rudeness.*

Robin scolds Rabbit.

Robin:

You've got to be nice.
Be sweet and say please,
Or we'll never see spring.
We'll just sit here and freeze.

We just need to wake him.
Let's ring this old bell.
Or maybe this horn
Will do just as well.

*Robin has props in
her pocket. She pulls
them out and rings
the bell at the hole
as she says her
lines.*

Rabbit:
Enough of this sweet talk
And being so nice.
I say we throw in
A bucket of ice.

Raindrops:
We'll grumble and groan
Right over his head.
We'll make enough noise
To wake up the dead.

Raindrops should say last two lines VERY LOUDLY. As raindrops are reciting, Butterfly enters.

Butterfly:
Maybe he's dead,
Or maybe it's worse.
He could be held under
An old witch's curse.

Butterfly should flutter as she says her lines.

Spring Chicken:
We have not seen a witch
In a year and a day.
I bet the gypsies
Took her away.

Spring Chicken enters. She speaks in a high "baby-like" voice.

Rabbit:
Forget about witches,
Gypsies, and clocks.
Let's fill up his hole
With pebbles and rocks.

Rabbit, with hands on hips, says first two lines. Then rubbing his hands together (devilishly) says last two lines. Pig enters as Rabbit recites.

Pig:
Throw him some candy,
Some burgers, and fries.
I'll bet he's just starved
For sodas and pies.

Pig looks in hole then recites lines to other characters.

Robin:

Let's go into his hole
On a rope with a light—
Just to make sure
That old Max is all right.

Robin appeals to all as she says her lines.

Raindrops:

Drizzle, Drazzle,
Plinkity, plet!
We drop from the skies
Until everything's wet.

Raindrops recite their lines. The characters all huddle and shiver under their umbrellas.

Narrator:

So they went off to find
Some rope and a light.
Max came out of his hole
As they moved out of sight.

All characters exit in same direction pantomiming conversation.

Max comes out as characters exit.

Max:

All I am to them
Is just a weatherman.
They come around once a year
To hear the weather plan.

Max is sad as he recites his lines. Max has an umbrella too.

They don't really like me.
I don't get asked to play
Or invited to a party
When it's someone's birthday.

I get really lonely, and
Sometimes I feel mad.
But most of the time
I feel very, very sad.

On the last two lines of the third stanza Max begins to cry. He cries into a towel.

Narrator:

Then poor Max cried
Such a lonesome sound
That the others came running,
And they gathered all around.

Direct Max to soften his sobs so the narrator can be heard. Characters re-enter.

Raindrops:

Grrr-umble, Rrrr-umble,
Zap, zap, ker-zip!
We're the April showers.
We go drip, drip, drip.

Characters gather around Max as the raindrops recite.

Rabbit:

First he makes us wait
While he oversleeps.
He won't look for his shadow.
He just sits there and weeps.

Robin:

We all tried to wake you.
We feared you were dead,
Or cursed by a witch,
Or bopped on the head.

Robin shakes her finger at Rabbit and shakes her head in disgust, then recites to Max. Max looks surprised at her concern.

Pig:

I knew you'd be hungry,
So I brought you this—
A lunch packed with goodies
And sealed with a kiss.

Pig hands Max the paper bag, looking very pleased with himself. Max is touched and smiles.

Butterfly:

Let's dry up those tears.
Use the tip of my wing.
We don't want a sad Max
When we're so close to spring.

Butterfly extends one wing and offers it to Max as she says her lines.

**Spring
Chicken:**

We're so glad to see you.
It's nice that you're here.
Now what can we do
To bring you some cheer?

*Spring Chicken says
lines in a high
"baby-like" voice.
Max smiles a big
smile for the first
time.*

Max:

I didn't think you liked me,
And so I made you wait.
I just wanted to be friends.
I hope it's not too late.

*As Max says his
lines he moves
forward so the
characters can
gather behind him in
a half circle. Rabbit
goes along with the
group, reluctantly.*

Rabbit:

There—I see it!
I knew it! I knew it!
A shadow! A shadow!
You blew it! You blew it!

*Rabbit jumps up and
down, VERY excited.
Rabbit is pointing at
the ground. All the
characters are
looking.*

Robin:

That's not his shadow
You silly old rabbit!
You get too excited.
It's a very bad habit.

*Robin shakes her
finger at Rabbit as
she recites. Rabbit
calms down and
joins the others as
they look.*

Narrator:

They looked, and they looked
Next to Max on the ground.
But there wasn't a trace
Of a shadow around.

*Characters all look
very happy when
they don't see a
shadow.*

*Narrator removes
scarf, hat and gloves
then turns his or her
umbrella around when
everyone else does.*

Raindrops:

Blossoming, blossoming—
It's the end of our showers.
Now is the time
To bring you May flowers.

*Raindrops open up
their raindrop props
and transform
themselves into the
spring flowers. At the
same time the
characters all turn
their umbrellas
around to reveal the
rainbows.*

Max:

Next year, my new friends,
You won't have to wait.
I'll show up on time.
Spring will not be late.

*Max says his lines as
all his new friends
gather around him.
The narrator(s) move
in at this time and
join the group.*

All:

Spring is all rainbows,
Flowers and such,
A time to make new friends
You like very much.

*All recite the final
stanza.*

Narrator:

The month is April.
There are clouds in the sky.
Shhh! - listen. You can hear
The rain if you try.

You see, Max is a groundhog
Who has the say-so,
As to the time
That winter will go.

He spends all winter long
In the ground fast asleep.
Then on February second
He comes up for a peek.

He comes out of his hole
And looks all around
To see if his shadow
Appears on the ground.

If he sees his shadow,
Winter will stay.
If there isn't a shadow,
Then spring's on the way.

So they went off to find
Some rope and a light.
Max came out of his hole
As they moved out of sight.

Then poor Max cried
Such a lonesome sound
That the others came running,
And they gathered all around.

They looked, and they looked
Next to Max on the ground.
But there wasn't a trace
Of a shadow around.

Spring is all rainbows,
Flowers and such,
A time to make new friends
You like very much.

Raindrops:

Grrr-umble, Rrrr-umble,
Zap, zap, ker-zip!
We're the April showers.
We go drip, drip, drip.

We'll grumble and groan
Right over his head.
We'll make enough noise
To wake up the dead.

Drizzle, Drazzle,
Plinkity, plet!
We drop from the skies
Until everything's wet.

Blossoming, blossoming -
It's the end of our showers.
Now is the time
To bring you May flowers.

Spring is all rainbows,
Flowers and such,
A time to make new friends
You like very much.

Take-Home Practice Script
Dear Parent - Please help your child learn these lines for a class play. Thank you.

Butterfly:

Maybe he's dead,
Or maybe it's worse.
He could be held under
An old witch's curse.

Let's dry up those tears.
Use the tip of my wing.
We don't want a sad Max
When we're so close to spring.

Spring is all rainbows,
Flowers and such,
A time to make new friends
You like very much.

Robin:

There may be no spring
At all this year.
We're still waiting
For old Max to appear.

This year we think
His alarm didn't ring.
Old Max overslept.
Now we're late for spring.

If these showers continue
Day after day,
We'll all surely drown
And be washed away.

You've got to be nice.
Be sweet and say please,
Or we'll never see spring.
We'll just sit here and freeze.

We just need to wake him.
Let's ring the old bell.
Or maybe this horn
Will do just as well.

Let's go into his hole
On a rope with a light -
Just to make sure
That old Max is all right.

We all tried to wake you.
We feared you were dead,
or cursed by a witch,
Or bopped on the head.

That's not his shadow
You silly old rabbit!
You get too excited.
It's a very bad habit.

Spring is all rainbows,
Flowers and such,
A time to make new friends
You like very much.

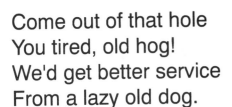

Rabbit:

Come out of that hole
You tired, old hog!
We'd get better service
From a lazy old dog.

Enough of this sweet talk
And being so nice.
I say we throw in
A bucket of ice.

Forget about witches,
Gypsies, and clocks.
Let's fill up his hole
With pebbles and rocks.

First he makes us wait
While he ovesleeps.
He won't look for his shadow.
He just sits there and weeps.

There - I see it!
I knew it! I knew it!
A shadow! A shadow!
You blew it! You blew it!

Spring is all rainbows,
Flowers and such,
A time to make new friends
You like very much.

Take-Home Practice Script
Dear Parent - Please help your child learn
these lines for a class play. Thank you.

**Spring
Chicken:**

We have not seen a witch
In a year and a day.
I bet the gypsies
Took her away.

We're so glad to see you.
It's nice that you're here.
Now what can we do
To bring you some cheer?

Spring is all rainbows,
Flowers and such,
A time to make new friends
You like very much.

Pig:

Throw him some candy,
Some burgers, and fries.
I'll bet he's just starved
For sodas and pies.

I knew you'd be hungry,
So I brought you this -
A lunch packed with goodies
And sealed with a kiss.

Spring is all rainbows,
Flowers and such,
A time to make new friends
You like very much.

- -

Max:

All I am to them
Is just a weatherman.
They come around once a year
To hear the weather plan.

They don't really like me.
I don't get asked to play
Or invited to a party
When it's someone's birthday.

I get really lonely, and
Sometimes I feel mad.
But most of the time
I feel very, very sad.

I didn't think you liked me,
And so I made you wait.
I just wanted to be friends.
I hope it's not too late.

Next year, my new friends,
You won't have to wait.
I'll show up on time.
Spring will not be late.

Spring is all rainbows,
Flowers and such,
A time to make new friends
You like very much.

class:

presents the play

Spring Starts Here!

date:

time:

place:

Please join us!

Spring Starts Here!

Narrator:_____

Max:_____

Robin:_____

Rabbit:_____

Butterfly:_____

Pig:_____

Spring Chicken:_____

Raindrops:

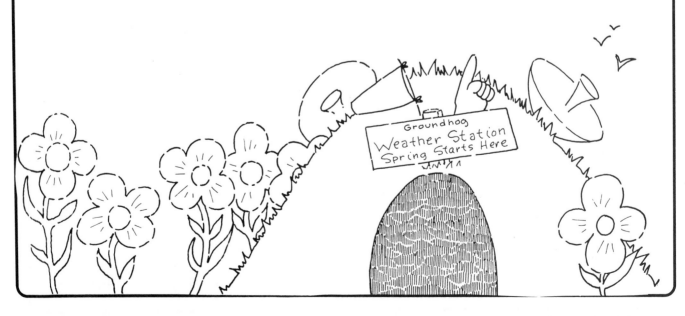

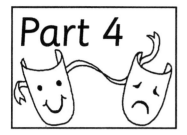

Part 4

Favorite Folktales

Everyone-Has-a-Part Plays

You don't need to avoid presenting a play simply because you have a large class. These plays provide parts for up to 30 students. Some are individual speaking parts, others are parts in small choruses. Shorter parts can be combined if you have a smaller class.

We provide everything you need to get started:

- Staging and scenery suggestions
- Costume ideas
- Lists of simple props
- Invitation to the play
- Program form listing cast members

Read through each play to help you decide which are appropriate for your students. Don't view some plays as too simple for older students. They have been successfully presented by older students for young audiences.

Rhyming Plays
in
Part 4

Things Could Always Be Worse (Yiddish Folktale) **189**

The Magic Pasta Pot (Italian Folktale) **217**

The Shoemaker and the Elves (German Folktale) **237**

Things Could Always Be Worse

A Yiddish Folktale
retold by Ginny Hall

Scenery	190
Characters and Costumes	192
Props	194
Script	195
Masks	208
Invitation	214
Play Program	215

Scenery

THE HOUSE

2 refrigerator boxes
white butcher paper
paint and brushes

Both side walls of the house are formed by slitting open the
refrigerator boxes and removing the top flaps. Cut a door that is
hinged on the left side.

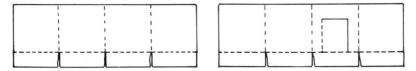

Select an alert sound effects person to bang two blocks together
each time Rubin closes the door. If all else fails, use a bell on the
door.

Stretch sheets of butcher paper between refrigerator boxes for the
back wall.

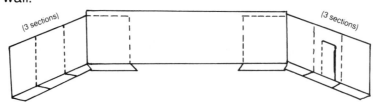

(3 sections)   (3 sections)

                                       How to Do Plays with Children

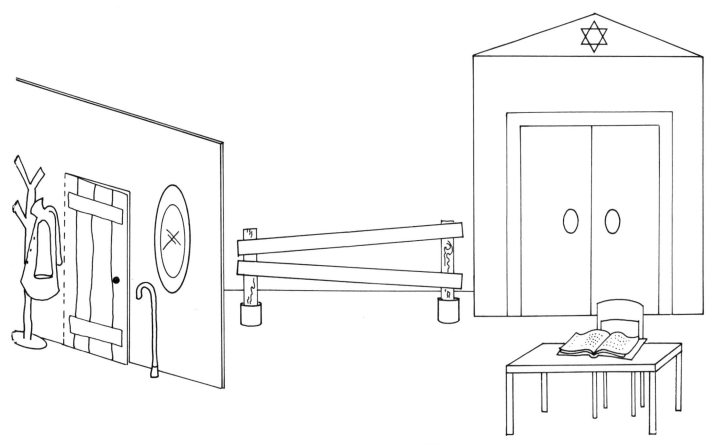

THE FENCE

Cut strips of cardboard and tape or staple together to form two long strips. Attach each end to a piece of lumber stuck in a coffee can full of sand. The animals wil stand behind this fence.

SYNAGOGUE

Attach butcher paper to a rolling chalkboard and paint a double door for the synagogue.

FINISHING TOUCHES

Beds—The beds are tables covered with blankets. Under each table is another bed on the floor.

Stove—The stove can be a large cardboard box painted to look like a stove. Cut a door in the box so Rachel can open the oven and take out bagels. Paint a stovepipe on the wall behind the stove.

Furnishings—Place throw rugs in the house. Pictures on the walls of the house are nice too. Flower pots or potted plants in the yard add color. Paint a mirror for Ita and the fireplace on the butcher paper. Paint a window with curtains by the fireplace.

Characters and Costumes

RUBIN — Rubin is a rather impatient person. He grumbles a lot and complains more. He is unhappy most of the time.

RABBI — The rabbi is wise and old. He moves slowly and thinks slowly. The beard will be longer than the beards of the other men.

    clothes like other men
    skull cap or tall black hat
    long black coat
    long beard
    glasses optional

MOLKA AND HANNAH — These ladies are very old. They are hunched over and walk slowly and carefully. Molka is wise and Hannah is snappy.

    glasses
    dress as other women do
    walking stick for Molka

MEN AND BOYS
white shirts
dark, baggy pants
vests if possible
boots
caps or bowler hats
beards — cut an elongated half-circle strip of paper and cover with cotton or yarn. Attach to the inside of hats and caps.

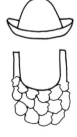

WOMEN AND GIRLS
long, plain, dark skirts or dresses
shawls
scarves wrapped around head
  and tied at the back of the neck
plain blouses

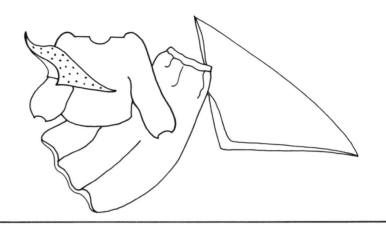

ANIMALS

If you are full of energy and would like to have more than masks for the animals—

PIG
This child crawls while wearing a
sleeved pink shirt and pink pants
(or all white). Make a paper spiral
tail and line it with a pipe cleaner
to support the paper. Pin it onto
the pants.

ROOSTER AND CHICKENS
Make wings of crepe paper. Cut it
the length of child's outstretched
arms and fold in half lengthwise.
Cut a hole for the child's head.
Round the outside corners
curving up from the body to the
outstretched hands. Staple
together at the bottom.

CAT AND DOG
Attach cat and dog ears to
headbands or caps. Have the
children wear all one color. Attach
a paper or yarn tail to each
animal. Put socks on their hands.

COW
Two children can be the cow, one
front end, one back end. Make the
body cover with an old sheet,
butcher paper, or a box. Paint
spots of brown or black on the
body and have children wear the
same color pants. Attach a
braided yarn tail to the back end.

193   How to Do Plays with Children

Props

★ MUSIC

Play music while the audience is seated and after the performance. "Fiddler on the Roof" is nice!

★ SCENERY PROPS

Check off

○ 8 blankets

○ 8 pillows

○ 1 tablecloth

○ 2 pots for stove

○ 3 platters or plates for bagels

○ clothes to scatter around the house

○ 2 chairs (rockers if possible) for Sarah and Hannah

○ 3 tables for beds

○ 1 large dinner table

○ wood logs for fire

○ vase of flowers for table

○ straw (weeds are great)

○ coat rack if possible or hang Rubin's coat on the back of a chair

○ 2 benches for table or 7 chairs

★ OTHER PROPS

○ 1 ball or dreidel for children to play with

○ lots of bagels

○ 6 bowls

○ 6 spoons

○ comb for Ita

○ walking stick for Molka

○ coat for Rubin

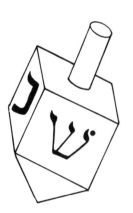

Things Could Always Be Worse
Script

Setting
The rabbi is sitting in the door of the synagogue carrying on a silent conversation with Estner and Abraham. All neighbor children are playing ball next to the synagogue. In the house, Daniel, Dora, and Mirrel are sitting at the table playing with bagels and banging their spoons. Rachel is serving bowls of cereal. Hannah is sleeping in a chair, snoring loudly. Ita is combing her hair. The house is messy. Clothes and blankets are all over. The cat and dog are fighting under the table. Rubin is sitting at the table, nearest the audience, eating a bagel. When he is finished, he places his hands over his ears. After a few moments he stands up.

Rubin: Silence! This noise is too much! Cats! Dogs! Children! This house is too crowded! It is driving me crazy!

Noise stops while Rubin is talking then continues when he is finished. Rubin walks in a small circle, in front of the table, his hands are over his ears. Daniel and Dora get up and follow, imitating him.

Rachel: Rubin, it is winter. It is too cold for the children to go outside and play. Our house is so small! It will always be noisy!

Rubin: I must do something! I cannot stay here a minute longer! I am going out! Goodbye!

Rubin puts on his coat. The door shuts. (Everyone in the house stops each time the door shuts. The characters in the house will stay in these positions until Rubin returns, so be sure they are comfortable.) Rubin trudges out and feeds straw to the cow. Noah and Molka enter, stage right, and walk over to Rubin.

Noah: Good morning, Rubin. How goes it with you?

Rubin: Ah! (heavy sigh) I am miserable. You do not know what it is like to live with so many people in one house. My children argue. My wife complains. My mother snores like a lion. The cat and dog fight. I never get a moment's peace. I do not know what to do.

Molka: Oh, you poor man. Families can be noisy, but they are a blessing.

Noah: You should go talk to the rabbi. He is a wise man. He'll know how to help you with your problems. Go! Ask the rabbi to help you.

Rubin: Things certainly could not be any worse! You are right. I shall go speak to him right now.

Noah and Molka exit stage right. Rubin walks to the synagogue. There he meets Estner and Abraham.

Estner: Good morning, Rubin!

Abraham: Isn't it a lovely day?

Rubin: Maybe for you. Life is miserable for me. My children argue. My wife complains. My mother snores like a lion. The cat and the dog fight. Things could not be worse!

Estner: Poor Rubin! You need a miracle!

Rubin: That would help. I am here to talk to our beloved rabbi. Maybe he can make a miracle.

Abraham: Well, good luck, Rubin.

Estner: Our beloved rabbi will help, you'll see. He is a very wise man. Good luck, Rubin.

Abraham: Come children. We must go now.

Estner, Freda, Mikhel, and Abraham exit behind synagogue. Freda and Mikhel wave good-bye to the other children.

Rabbi: Good day, Rubin. How are things with your family today?

Rubin: Rabbi, you must help me! My house is a terrible place. It is too small. The children argue. My wife complains. My mother snores like a lion. The cat and the dog fight. I am a good man. I do not deserve this. What am I to do?

Rabbi: This does not sound good. But I think I can help you. Do you have any chickens?

He thinks, stroking his beard.

Rubin: Yes, I have chickens. How can they help?

Rabbi: Do not question what I say. Follow my instructions. Bring all your chickens into your house.

Rubin walks away from the Rabbi scratching his head and looking puzzled. He goes behind the fence. He shoos the chickens around the corner and into the house. He hangs up his coat. The chickens are clucking loudly all the time. Rebekah, Jakob, and Jonah watch Rubin. When he goes into the house, they run to the window and peek in.

Rubin: Yes, Rabbi, I shall do as you say.

Rachel: What are you doing Rubin? Why are you bringing the chickens into the house? Have you gone mad?

Ita: Papa! The chickens will mess up our house!

Rubin: Ita, do not question me. Our beloved rabbi has told me to do this!

The chickens walk around the house. Each finds a place, settles in, and clucks loudly. The children argue. Hannah snores. The cat and dog fight. Rebekah, Jakob, and Jonah run off, stage right, laughing. Rubin gets a bowl of cereal and sits at the table. Rubin puts his hands over his ears and lays his head down on the table. He falls asleep. The children and Rachel go to their beds and go to sleep. Lights go off.

Rooster: Cock-a-doodle-doo!
Cock-a-doodle-doo!

Lights go on. Hannah is snoring loudly. After a few moments, the chickens begin to cluck. After a few moments, the children wake up and begin to argue. Rachel wakes up and begins putting food on the table. Rubin wakes up. Rubin looks around the room. He stands up. The cat and dog begin to fight.

Rubin: Silence! This is terrible! What good has it done to bring the chickens into the house? I must go ask the rabbi what to do.

Everyone stops for a moment. Then the noise resumes. Rubin puts on his coat. He walks out the door. (Noise stops.) He grumbles on his way back to the synagogue.

Rabbi: Rubin, how are things at your house?

Rubin: Rabbi, Rabbi, you must help me. The children still argue. My wife still complains. My mother still snores like a lion. The cat and the dog still fight. AND NOW the chickens cluck, cluck, cluck. There was enough noise before. I am a good man. I do not deserve this. You must help me.

Rabbi: Ah, Rubin. Do you have a rooster?

He thinks, stroking his beard.

Rubin:	Yes, I have a grand rooster!	*Rubin says proudly.*
Rabbi:	Then bring the rooster into your house.	
Rubin:	Rabbi, are you sure that will help?	
Rabbi:	Do not question me, Rubin! Do as I say.	*Rubin walks home, shaking his head and muttering. He goes behind the fence and chases the rooster around the front and into the house. The rooster gets up on the table and begins to crow. Rubin hangs up his coat.*
Rooster:	Cock-a-doodle-doo! Cock-a-doodle-doo!	*The chickens cluck. The children argue. Hannah snores. The cat and dog fight. Rubin sits down at the table and puts his head in his hands. Hannah wakes up and hobbles to Rubin.*
Hannah:	Rubin, why have you brought the rooster into the house? Do we not have enough noise? You must take it outside!	
Rubin:	I do not need your advice too. Our beloved rabbi told me to bring the rooster into the house. So the rooster shall stay.	
Rachel:	Yes, our beloved rabbi is a wise man. We must follow his advice.	*Daniel, Mirrel, and Dora start to chase the rooster. Rubin watches. The rooster goes back to the table. Rubin goes outside and brings in some wood. He sits down at the table and watches. After a minute he falls asleep. Everyone goes to sleep as before. Lights go off.*

 How to Do Plays with Children

Rooster: Cock-a-doodle-doo!
Cock-a-doodle-doo!

Lights go on. Hannah is snoring loudly. After a few moments, the chickens begin to cluck. The children wake up and begin to argue. Rachel gets up. The cat and dog begin to fight. Rubin wakes up. Rachel begins putting food on the table. Rubin looks around the room awhile. He stands up.

Rubin: Silence! Stop chasing the rooster! The squawking is terrible! What should I do? I must go see the rabbi. Maybe he has made a mistake.

The noise stops for a moment then resumes. Rubin puts on his coat. He walks out the door. (Noise stops.) Rubin walks slowly back to the rabbi.

Rubin: Rabbi, my house is a mess. You must help me! The children still argue. My wife still complains. My mother still snores like a lion. The cat and dog still fight. The chickens cluck, cluck, cluck. AND NOW the rooster cock-a-doodle-doos! I am a good man! I do not deserve this! You must help me.

Rabbi: Ah, Rubin. Do you have a cow and a pig? *He thinks, stroking his beard.*

Rubin: Yes, I have a cow and a pig. What do you want me to do? Surely you would not ask me to bring them in the house too?

Rabbi: Yes, you must take the cow and the pig into the house. Do not question me, just do as I say!

Rubin slowly walks back to the house shaking and scratching his head. He leads the cow into the house. He hangs up his coat.

Rubin: Daniel, bring the pig and the cow in the house.

Daniel: Bring the pig and the cow in the house?

Rubin: Yes, Daniel. Bring the pig and the cow
in the house!

Daniel: Yes, Papa.

*Daniel goes outside
and pushes the pig
and the cow into the
house.*

Dora: Oh boy! All the animals are in the house now.

Mirrel: Oh, Papa! Thank you for bringing Curly in the
house. It is too cold outside for my Curly.

*Mirrel runs to Curly and
hugs him. Curly oinks
loudly and runs away.
Mirrel chases him, trying
to hug him. The cow
walks to the fireplace and
begins to moo.*

Daniel: Papa, Papa, can I sleep with Curly tonight?
Please! Please!

Rubin: Yes, yes, now be quiet!

Rachel: Rubin, you must get some straw if we are to
have these animals in the house.

Rubin: Yes, Rachel, I will go get some straw.

*Rubin goes outside to get
the straw. Molka hobbles
over to him.*

Molka: How are things with you now, Rubin? Did our
beloved rabbi help?

Rubin: Things are terrible! I do not understand the
rabbi's advice.

Molka: Our beloved rabbi is a very wise man. He has a
plan. Things will get better. Have patience, Rubin.

*Molka leaves. Rubin
takes the straw into the
house and puts it near
the fire. The cow moos
and walks over and eats
some. Rubin sits down
at the table and eats
another bagel. After a
moment he holds his
head in his hands.*

Ita: Papa, why did you bring this cow in the house?

Hannah gets up and walks over to Rubin.

Hannah: My Rubin, you are a crazy man. This house smells and the noise is terrible. Why are you doing this?

Rubin: Our beloved rabbi has told me to. He is a wise man. We must not question his advice.

Hannah shrugs, goes back to her chair, and begins to snore. Rubin listens to the noise. He sits down at the table, and soon he falls asleep. Everyone goes to sleep as before.

Rooster: Cock-a-doodle-doo! Cock-a-doodle-doo!

Lights go on. Hannah is snoring loudly. After a few moments, the chickens begin to cluck. After a few moments the children wake up and begin to argue. Rachel gets up. The cat and dog begin to fight. Rachel begins serving food. Rubin wakes up and watches. The cow walks to the table and begins eating the food. The pig goes after the dog. Daniel and Dora chase the pig.

Rachel: Quiet! This is too much! I cannot stand all this noise. Cluck, cluck, cluck, oink, oink, oink, moo, moo, moo. Rubin, you must go to the rabbi. He has surely made a mistake.

Rubin: Ah, Rachel, I agree. Our beloved rabbi must have made a mistake. I will go speak to him.

Noise stops for a moment then begins again. Rubin puts on his coat. He walks out the door. (Noise stops.) He walks to the rabbi.

Rabbi: Ah, Rubin. I am glad to see you. How are things today?

Rubin: Rabbi, Rabbi. I am miserable! The children still argue. My wife still complains. My mother still snores like a lion. The cat and dog still fight. The chickens cluck, cluck, cluck. The rooster cock-a-doodle-doos! AND NOW the cow moos, and the pig oinks. I am a good man! I do not deserve this! What am I to do?

Rabbi: Ah, Rubin. Do you have any relatives that live nearby?

He thinks, stroking his beard.

Rubin: My wife's brother Heime and his wife Sarah live near.

Rabbi: Then go invite them to come to your house. Ask them to stay.

Rubin: But, Rabbi, there is no room!

Rabbi: Do not question my advice. Go and do as I say!

Rubin walks behind the house. Mikhel, Freda and Estner enter stage right. Mikhel and Freda are pulling Estner by the hands.

Mikhel: Mama, you must come see. Rubin has put all the animals in the house. Come and see.

Estner: Mikhel, you are right. Poor Rachel! How can she stand all the mess and the smell?

(surprised)

Freda: Mama, can we bring all the animals into our house too? They are so cold outside.

Estner: No! Come children, we must go home. I cannot stand the smell! Come now!

Estner takes Mikhel and Freda by the hand and takes them off stage behind the synagogue. Rubin enters with Heime, Sarah, and Hershel following him. They enter the house. Rachel rushes to greet them and hugs each one. Rubin hangs up his coat.

Rachel: Oh, Heime and Sarah, it is so good to see you! It has been such a long time since we have talked, dear Brother. Come sit down. I will fix you some supper. Rubin, you have made me so happy!

Heime: I am so hungry. What are we having for supper?

Sarah: This house is a mess! Where am I to sit?

Hershel: I hate animals! Why are the animals in the house? It stinks!

Ita: Our beloved rabbi has told Papa to bring them in. The house does stink. It is crazy!

Heime and Hershel sit down at the table. Sarah sits in a chair next to Hannah and starts snoring. Rachel puts food on the table. Heime and Hershel put all the food in front of them and begin eating. The children watch. The cow goes to the table and tries to eat some food. Hershel pushes it away.

Heime: Rachel, do you have more bagels? I am so hungry.

Hershel: I want some halvah!

How to Do Plays with Children

Rachel: I will make some for you. I will hurry.

Rachel rushes to put more food on the table. Noah, Abraham, and Rebekah walk over and look in the window. They walk to front center stage. The noise in the house continues but at a lower volume.

Noah: Rubin must be crazy!

Abraham: I do not understand why he has invited Heime and Sarah to his house.

Noah: Heime and Hershel will eat everything in the house.

Abraham: And Sarah does nothing but complain and snore.

Rebekah: Papa, Papa, can I go play with Dora? What fun to have a pig in the house!

Abraham: Come. There is too much noise, even out here. Let us go back to the peace and quiet of our homes.

Noah takes Rebekah's hand, and they all leave. Sarah wakes up and walks over to Rubin.

Sarah: I cannot sleep with all this noise! Rubin, you must take these animals outside.

Heime: And I cannot eat with that cow in the house!

Rachel: Hershel, are you still hungry?

Hershel: Yes! Where is my halvah? Bring it quickly!

Rachel stands at the stove. Heime continues to eat and Sarah chases the pig. The pig hides under the bed. Rubin sits down at the table and begins to sob loudly. He stands up and shouts.

Rubin: Silence! I cannot stand this any longer! I must go ask our beloved rabbi for advice.

Everyone stops for a moment. Then noise resumes. Rubin puts on his coat. He walks out the door. He walks to the rabbi, still sobbing.

Rabbi: Ah, Rubin. I am so glad to see you. How are things at your house?

Rubin: Rabbi, what shall I do? Life is miserable! The children still argue. My wife still complains. My mother still snores like a lion. The chickens cluck, cluck, cluck. The rooster cock-a-doodle-doos. The cow moos. The pig oinks. AND NOW Heime and Hershel eat all the food in the house, and Sarah complains too.

Rabbi: Ah, Rubin. Then it is time to send Heime and his family home. Go and tell them all to leave. Take the cow and pig back to the barn. Put the rooster and the chickens out. Go now and do as I say!

Rubin walks slowly home. He walks in the door. The noise resumes. He hangs up his coat.

Rubin: Silence! Heime, it is time to say good-bye. We have no more food!

Everyone stops.

Hershel: No more food! Papa, we must go home. I am still hungry.

Heime: Come, Sarah and Hershel. We must go find something to eat.

Heime, Sarah, and Hershel leave in a huff.

Rubin: Daniel, take the cow to the barn. Dora, you take the pig. Ita and Mirrel, shoo the chickens out. I will take the rooster.

Everyone takes the animals out. The animals all make appropriate noises as they leave. Daniel, Dora, Mirrel, Ita, and Rubin all return to the house. Daniel, Dora, and Mirrel sit down at the table. They eat their bagels and bang their spoons (quietly). Rachel cleans up the straw. Hannah and Ita clean the table. Hannah goes back to her chair and starts snoring (softly). Ita is combing her hair. The cat and dog are fighting quietly under the table. Rubin sits down at the table and eats a bagel. He keeps looking around, smiling.

Rubin: My house is the most wonderful, cozy house in the village! Our beloved rabbi is a very, very wise man!

Hannah wakes up and walks to Rubin.

Hannah: I cannot stand this noise. Rubin, you must make them stop.

Rubin stands up and smiles.

Rubin: Ah, Hannah, this is heaven! *(Pause.)* Things could ALWAYS be worse!

CURTAIN

Reproduce this pattern on card stock.

1. Color the mask.
2. Cut on the dotted line.
3. Tape a tongue depressor handle to the mask.

How to Do Plays with Children

Pig Mask

1. Color the mask.
2. Cut on the dotted line.
3. Tape a tongue depressor handle to the mask.

How to Do Plays with Children

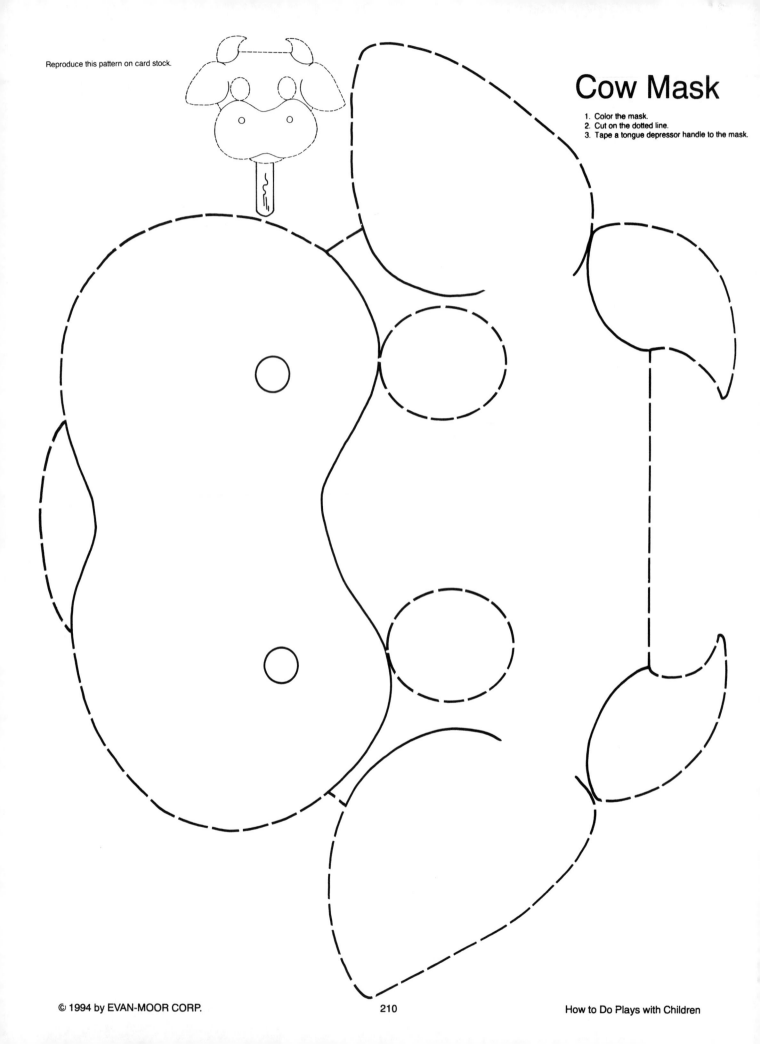

Reproduce this pattern on card stock.

Cow Mask

1. Color the mask.
2. Cut on the dotted line.
3. Tape a tongue depressor handle to the mask.

210

How to Do Plays with Children

Reproduce this pattern on card stock.

Rooster
Mask

1. Color the mask.
2. Cut on the dotted line.
3. Tape a tongue depressor handle to the mask.

How to Do Plays with Children

Reproduce this pattern on card stock.

Dog Mask

1. Color the mask.
2. Cut on the dotted line.
3. Tape a tongue depressor handle to the mask.

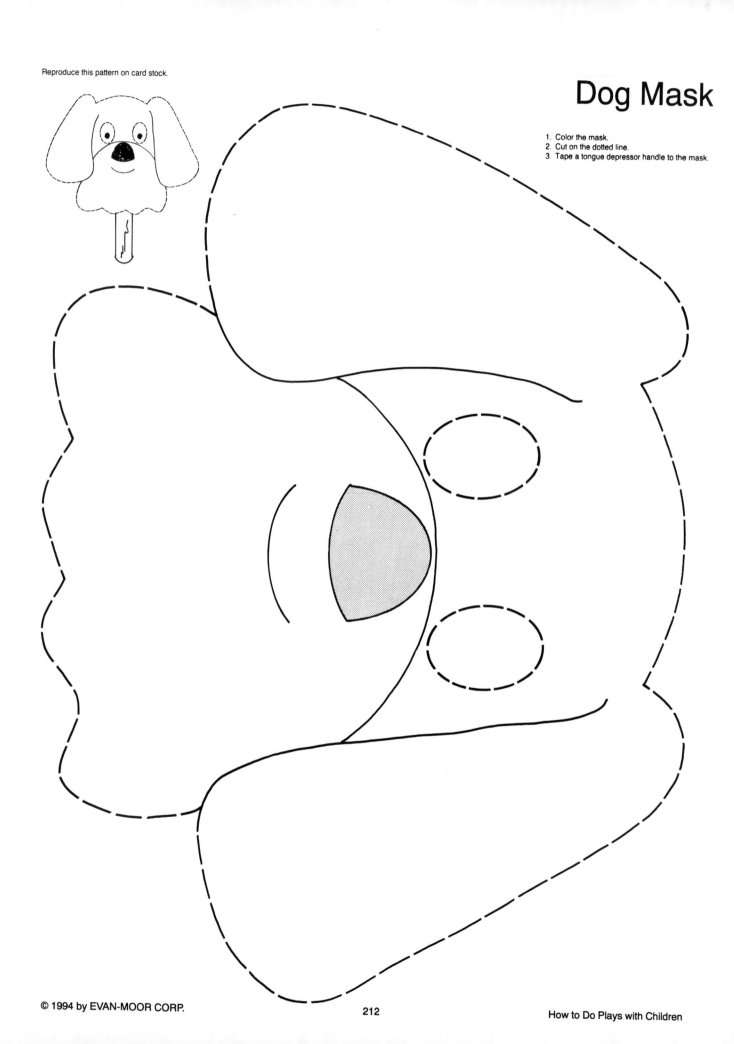

Cat Mask

1. Color the mask.
2. Cut on the dotted line.
3. Tape a tongue depressor handle to the mask.

213

How to Do Plays with Children

class:

presents the play

Things
Could Always
Be Worse

date:

time:

place:

Please join us!

Things Could Always Be Worse

Cast

Rabbi _____   Rachel _____

Heime _____   Hannah _____

Sarah _____   Ita _____

Hershel _____   Daniel _____

Mirrel _____   Dora _____

Rubin _____

Neighbors

Abraham _____

Estner _____

Noah _____

Molka _____

Neighbor Children

Rebekah _____

Jakob _____

Jonah _____

Freda _____

Mikhel _____

Animals

Dog _____

Rooster _____

Cow _____

Cat _____

Pig _____

Chickens

_____

_____

_____

_____

_____

How to Do Plays with Children

Name _____

How Many Words Can You Make?

Using only the letters in the boxed words, make as many words as you can.

| miserable | | fireplace | |

_____ _____   _____ _____

_____ _____   _____ _____

_____ _____   _____ _____

_____ _____   _____ _____

_____ _____   _____ _____

_____ _____   _____ _____

_____ _____   _____ _____

| understand | | relatives | |

_____ _____   _____ _____

_____ _____   _____ _____

_____ _____   _____ _____

_____ _____   _____ _____

_____ _____   _____ _____

_____ _____   _____ _____

The Magic Pasta Pot

An Italian Folktale
retold by Ginny Hall

Scenery 218

Characters and Costumes 220

Props 222

Script 224

Invitation 235

Play Program 236

Scenery

Paint curtains.

Table covered with paper.

WELCOME

ZINGARELLA'S HOUSE

- Use two refrigerator boxes to make Zingarella's house. Remove the tops and bottoms from the boxes. Cut along one side of each box, open out (like a folding screen or room divider), and tape the two boxes together along one side.

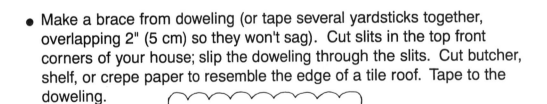

- Make a brace from doweling (or tape several yardsticks together, overlapping 2" (5 cm) so they won't sag). Cut slits in the top front corners of your house; slip the doweling through the slits. Cut butcher, shelf, or crepe paper to resemble the edge of a tile roof. Tape to the doweling.

- Cut a window in Zingarella's house. It must be large so Luigi can be seen looking through it.
- Paint the top cupboards. Use a table for the lower ones, putting on a painted paper false front.
- Furnish Zingarella's house with playhouse furniture from the kindergarten or tables and chairs from your classroom.
- Place a row of potted plants and a welcome mat across the front of your "house."

  If you cannot get refrigerator boxes, use a puppet theater covered with painted background to create Zingarella's house.

PIAZZA

Rolling chalkboards are good to hang scenery on! You can move it easily and quickly. Scenery can also be hung on paint easels.

Butcher paper is the largest, easiest, and cheapest way to make scenery. Use lots of paint too!

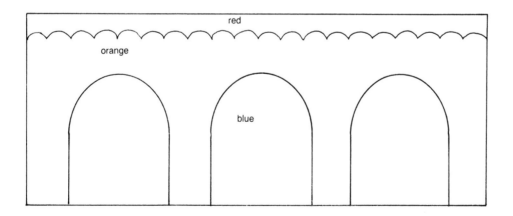

Sometimes it is more effective (and easier) to cut large things, such as windows and doors, from colored butcher paper; then glue it on the background.

How to Do Plays with Children

Characters and Costumes

ZINGARELLA is a wise and kind woman. She is plump (use pillows front and back) and always wears a scarf and a shawl. She has a long skirt and sturdy shoes. She is always hunched over, for she is getting old.

LUIGI is not very bright. He is very clumsy and is always tripping and bumping into everything. He talks slowly and loves to play with the children. He always wears a funny hat, big boots, short pants, and a shirt that is never tucked in.

BENITO is a loveable cat. She purrs loudly and flicks her tail a great deal. The costume can be black tights, a black leotard, and a black cotton tube stuffed with fiberfill. A clear thread can be attached near the end of the tail. The other end of the thread is held in the cat's hand so that the tail can be pulled up and down.

MICHAELANGELO, the painter, wears a beret and smock covered with different colors of paint. He carries a paint brush and palette.

The SOLDIER wears a hat and a sash with a sword attached at the waist. The sword can be cut out of cardboard and painted.

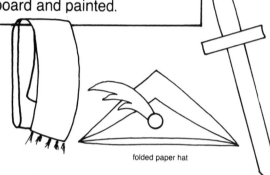

folded paper hat

The WOMEN wear long skirts or dresses. They may wear shawls and jewelry. The shawls can be created by folding square tablecloths diagonally.

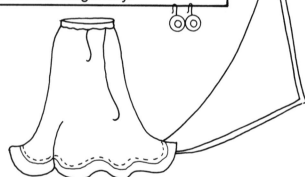

The MEN wear pants and peasant-type clothing if possible. Some wear hats.

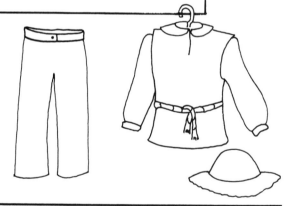

The CHILDREN dress similarly to the adults. The girls might wear flowers or ribbons in their hair. The boys can wear short pants.

paper bag vest

How to Do Plays with Children

Props

Check off

○ 1. an easel with the Mona Lisa on it

○ 2. paint brush and palette

○ 3. basket or crate for the fish and vegetables

○ 4. two tables, one as a dinner table in the house, one as a cupboard

○ 5. table cloth

○ 6. jars with colored liquid (orange soda)

○ 7. cloth with concealed pin

○ 8. balloon ½ blown up as wart

○ 9. rug

○ 10. bucket for water

○ 11. hammer and nail

○ 12. large fork

○ 13. paper plates, plastic forks for villagers

○ 14. plastic glasses in cupboard

○ 15. blankets, pillows to block pasta

○ 16. 2 chairs for table

How to Do Plays with Children

○ 17. vegetables for basket–These can be real or made of plastic or papier-mâché.

○ 18. fish for basket–These can be created by cutting out two fish shapes exactly the same size. Color or paint each one. Staple together leaving a space; stuff with crumpled newspapers. Staple the opening.

○ 19. cardboard sign–Cut a large piece of cardboard from a box. Paint.

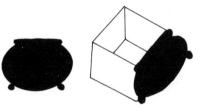

HELP WANTED
Work in garden
and house
FREE food
and
warm bed
See Zingarella

○ 20. pasta pot–Find a cardboard box large enough for a child to sit in. Cut a pot shape from black butcher paper. Make it large enough to cover the side of the box. Glue or staple to the front side of the box.

○ 21. pasta–Have your students make oodles of white paper chains, a few with narrow strips of paper, many with wider strips. Cut a piece of cardboard as wide as the mouth of the pasta pot. Glue some of the chains made from the narrow strips to the cardboard shape. The child inside the pot will hold this up when the pot makes pasta. The rest of the small chains are inside the pot (box) and will be served to the villagers by Luigi. The larger chains are also in the pot (box). The child inside will throw these out when the pot overflows.

How to Do Plays with Children

The Magic Pasta Pot

An Italian Folktale
Script

> **Setting:** *A piazza in Italy many years ago. Two children are watching Michelangelo painting at an easel. Anna is selling vegetables. Rosanna and Geno are buying vegetables. Vito is selling fish from a basket. Vincent, Leonardo, Anita, and Giorgio are talking to Vito. Mario, Giovanni, and Salvatore are talking to each other. Domenic, Francesca, Marco, and Katerina are walking around the piazza followed by extra children. Several children are playing ball. Zingarella is sweeping her kitchen. Benito, her cat, is sleeping in the corner. Maria enters stage right and walks over to Rosanna. Maria is holding her head.*

Maria: Oh! I have such a headache!
I think it will never go away.
What should I do?

Rosanna: You should go see Zingarella.
She can cure headaches with her
magic ways. Go! Go! Find Zingarella.
She will help you. Subito!

Maria walks to Zingarella's house and knocks on the door. Zingarella opens the door.

Zingarella: Buon giorno, Maria! Oh, poor Maria,
you look terrible. What is wrong,
my child?

Maria: Zingarella, please, can you help me?
I have such a headache! It won't go
away. Please, please, can you help me?

Zingarella: Come in child. Come in, sit down, and
rest yourself. I will mix a potion to cure your
headache. Soon it will be better.

Maria puts her head in her hands and moans as Zingarella goes to the cupboard, gets two jars, and pours their contents into a glass. She stirs the potion and hands it to Maria.

         How to Do Plays with Children

Zingarella: Here, poor child. Drink this and you will certainly feel better soon.

Maria drinks the potion and waits a few seconds. She jumps up and hugs Zingarella.

Maria: Zingarella, you are wonderful! You have cured my headache! You are magico, magico! Grazie, Grazie!

Zingarella: I am glad to help you, Maria. Now go and enjoy the day. Ciao.

Zingarella cleans up and starts sweeping as Maria goes out the door to the piazza. Pietro enters stage right. He has a balloon between his fingers (his wart). Maria and Pietro meet about center stage.

Maria: Poor, poor Pietro! What is wrong with your finger?

Pietro: Oh, Maria, I have a wart that grows bigger and bigger each day. I can no longer work in the fields. I do not know what to do. Maria, can you help me? What am I to do?

Maria: Oh, Pietro, you should go see Zingarella. She has just cured my headache. She can surely make your wart go away.

Pietro: Grazie, grazie, Maria. Maybe she <u>can</u> help me! I will go see her right away.

Pietro walks to Zingarella's house and knocks on the door. Zingarella opens the door.

Zingarella: Buon giorno, Pietro. I have not seen you in such a long time. You must be very busy harvesting your grapes now. Pietro, what is wrong with your finger?

Pietro: Oh, Zingarella, you must help me! This wart on my finger grows larger every day. I cannot work in my fields any longer. My family will surely starve if I do not pick my grapes soon. Can you make this wart go away? Please! You must help me! You must!

Pietro sits down at the table and cries. Benito gets up and goes over and rubs against Pietro's leg. Zingarella goes over and pats Pietro on the back.

Zingarella: Pietro, Pietro, do not cry. I will take your wart away. Let me get my magic cloth.

Zingarella goes to the cupboard and gets the cloth. Benito sits down and watches. Pietro watches as Zingarella gets the cloth. She walks back and places the cloth on the wart. (The pin inside punctures the balloon.) Pietro jumps up in surprise and looks at his finger.

Pietro: Zingarella, you are wonderful! You have cured me! You are an angel! You have saved my family from starving. Grazie!

Zingarella: Go now and pick your grapes, and give my love to your wife and children.

Pietro leaves and Zingarella cleans up and continues to sweep. Pietro walks through the piazza and off stage right. Benito plays with the broom as Zingarella sweeps. Giuseppe enters stage right moping. He walks across stage and leans against Zingarella's house. Zingarella walks out of the house and sees him standing there. She looks at him closely. He continues to look forlorn.

Zingarella: Giuseppe, what is the matter? I have never seen anyone look as sad as you do. Tell me what makes you so sad, Giuseppe?

Giuseppe: My heart is broken. Katerina will not speak to me. I think I will die of a broken heart.

Zingarella: I can fix that, Giuseppe. I will make a special potion, and Katerina will see she has made a terrible mistake. You wait here. I will be right back.

Zingarella goes into the house and takes a bottle out of the cupboard. She brings it out and hands it to Giusippe.

Zingarella: Here, drink a swallow of this. This will solve your problem, and then you will not die of a broken heart. Poor Giuseppe, life will soon be sweet again.

Giuseppe drinks a swallow of the potion. Benito charges out of the house and runs to Giuseppe and rubs and rubs against his legs. Giuseppe looks at Benito and smiles. He bends down and pets Benito.

Giuseppe: Well, it has certainly worked on Benito. Maybe it will work on Katerina also. Grazie, Zingarella. You have made me very hopeful. Grazie! Grazie!

Zingarella watches as Giuseppe walks to the piazza. Katerina sees him coming. She looks up shyly and he looks at her. He lifts his nose high in the air and walks off stage right as Katerina follows him eagerly. Zingarella goes back into the house shaking her head and sits down on the chair. Benito walks up to her and rubs against her and meows. She pets the cat and talks to it.

Zingarella: Oh, Benito, I am getting old. I am too old to work in the garden. My back hurts when I pick the zucchini. My eyes can no longer see the dust in the corners. I must find someone to help me. What to do? What to do? *(Pause)* I have it! I will make a sign and place it in the piazza. Surely there is someone who will help me. I will offer a warm bed and food.

Zingarella gets a piece of cardboard out of the cupboard and writes on it. She finishes and shows it to Benito.

Zingarella: There! What do you think? That looks good to me!

Benito sits up on hind legs and inspects the sign. He nods approval and watches as Zingarella goes out the door with hammer, nails, and sign. She walks to the piazza and nails the sign to the wall. She looks at the sign and walks back to her house, greeting those she passes along the way. She goes into the house and sits down at the table and falls asleep. Villagers read the sign as they walk by. Luigi enters stage right walking very slowly and bumping into things as he goes. He waves at the children. He sees the sign and walks over to it. He reads it out loud very slowly. He takes it off the wall and reads it again. (Out loud.) He looks towards Zingarella's house and scratches his head. He faces the audience.

Luigi: I can help work in the garden. I guess I can learn to clean a house. It couldn't be too hard. I'm so hungry, and everyone knows Zingarella makes the best pasta in town. A nice warm bed sounds good too. I am tired of sleeping in the stable on that itchy hay. I will go tell Zingarella I am the man for the job!

Luigi walks across stage slowly and bumps into everyone and everything. He knocks over the fish basket on his way and Vito shakes his head in exasperation. The children run up to him. One child is holding a ball.

Child 1: Buon giorno, Luigi. Do you want to play ball with us?

Luigi: I cannot play with you today, for I must go see Zingarella. She needs ME! I must help her do the work in the house and in the garden. Then I get to eat all the pasta I want. I will come and play with you when I have finished my work. Addio!

He arrives at the door and bangs on it. Zingarella wakes up with a start and answers the door. He straightens his shirt and stands tall.

Luigi: Luigi is here to help you in the garden and the house. *(He shoves the sign in her face.)* I am very strong and VERY hungry. Do you have some of your pasta for me?

Zingarella looks him up and down and walks slowly around him.

Zingarella: Hm-m-m. You must feed the animals and weed the garden. You must go to the well and fetch water every day if you want MY pasta.

Luigi: I will do all those things. I will even learn how to clean your house. What do you have to eat?

Zingarella hands him a bucket.

Zingarella: Here, go fetch water from the well first. Subito! I will make you something to eat while you are gone.

Luigi hurries to the well and gets the water. Zingarella takes a dish and fork out of the cupboard while he is gone. He returns, but goes behind the house and looks in the window. At that moment Zingarella goes to the pasta pot. He watches.

Zingarella:	Luigi will eat so much food. Oh, well, I have my pasta pot. I will fill him up with pasta. Bubble, bubble pasta pot. Make me pasta, nice and hot. Pasta's what I want for dinner. I don't want to get much thinner.	*When she finishes, the pot begins to bubble and boil. Slowly pasta starts to show at the top. Luigi watches in amazement. The pot contin-ues to bubble a few seconds longer.*
Zingarella:	That should be enough to fill him up. Stop, stop, pasta pot. I have my pasta, nice and hot. There's enough to fill me up, Until the morning sun comes up.	*At this point Luigi disappears. Zingarella jumps up and down three times, turns around three times, and kicks the pot three times. She counts each of these movements in Italian.*
Zingarella:	Uno, due, tre. Uno, due, tre. Uno, due, tre.	
Luigi:	This is wonderful! This is surely magico! I can be magic too. Oh boy, oh boy! I can make magico!	*He knocks at the door, Zingarella opens it.*
Zingarella:	Sit, sit, Luigi. I have made pasta. When you have finished, you must weed the garden and feed the animals. I must go visit my sick friend. I will be back later. And remember, DO NOT TOUCH THE PASTA POT!!! Do you hear me, Luigi?	
Luigi:	Si, si, I hear you. Zingarella. I will weed the garden and feed all the animals. I will not touch the pasta pot.	

Zingarella puts on her shawl and walks out the door. Luigi quickly eats the rest of his food, not taking his eyes off the pot. He gets up and walks around the pasta pot, look-ing at it carefully. He runs out the door and excitedly yells to the villagers.

Luigi:	I have a magic pasta pot! I can make pasta for everyone. I can make all the pasta you can eat. I can make it for the whole village.	*Everyone stops and looks at Luigi. They shake their heads in disbelief.*

Anna: There is no such thing as a magic pasta pot, Luigi! How silly you are!

Michelangelo: Luigi, you are crazy! Whoever heard of a magic pasta pot?!

Geno: You cannot even boil water, Luigi. How can you make pasta?

Children:	Luigi is a silly goose. The brains in his head are loose. Pasta doesn't grow in pots. Moms make pasta, lots and lots! Luigi is a silly goose. The brains in his head are loose.	*The children laugh and walk towards their parents. The villagers laugh and talk among themselves.*

Luigi:	You'll see! Go get your plates and forks, and come to Zingarella's house. I can make pasta as good as Zingarella's! Subito! Subito! Get your plates.	*The villagers shake their heads but go toward their houses to get plates and forks. Luigi returns to the house and stands over the pasta pot.*

Luigi:	Let's see. What did she say to make the pot work? Ah, I think it was, yes this was it..	
	Cook, cook, pasta pot. Make me pasta, nice and warm. Pasta's what I want for dinner. I don't want to be a thinker.	*Nothing happens. He scratches his head.*

Luigi: Maybe it was...

Bubble, bubble, pasta pot.
Make me pasta, nice and warm.
Pasta's what I want for dinner.
I don't want to get much...thinner!

He looks at the pot; nothing happens. He thinks for a moment.

Ah! I've got it!
Bubble, bubble, pasta pot.
Make me pasta, nice and hot.
Pasta's what I want for dinner.
I don't want to get much...thinner!

The pot begins to bubble and boil. Luigi watches it carefully, smiling. Pasta begins to show at the top of the pot. Luigi jumps up and down excitedly. He runs to the door and yells.

Luigi: Come and get your nice, hot pasta!
I did it! I did it! Come and see. I am
not a silly goose! I'm magico! Subito!
Subito! Come and see how smart I am!

The villagers and children come to the house and form a line. As they see the pasta, they cheer Luigi.

Vito: Luigi, you are truly amazing! You did it!
There is pasta in the pot, and it looks
GOOD!

Vincent: Luigi is our hero! He <u>can</u> cook after all.
He is a hero! Benissimo, Luigi!

Mario: You are not a fool, Luigi! We are sorry!
We have make a mistake. Luigi, you are
wonderful!

Anita: We will never go hungry again! Luigi is
our hero!

Luigi puts pasta on the plates, and the villagers go to the piazza to eat. Pasta continues to appear at the top until the last person is served. The villagers continue talking as each plate is filled.

       How to Do Plays with Children

Leonarda: We should never have doubted you, Luigi! You are terrifico! Benissimo! Benissimo!

After all the people have been served and are in the piazza, the pot continues to boil and Luigi, looking very pleased with himself, looks at the pot.

Giorgio: Grazie! Grazie!

Children: We love pasta! Luigi has made pasta for all of us! Grazie, Luigi, grazie!

Luigi: That is enough! I remember what she said to stop the pot!

Stop, stop, pasta pot.
I have my pasta, nice and hot.
There's enough to fill me up,
Until the next sun goes down.

He watches the pot, and it continues to boil. The pasta gets higher. Luigi walks around and watches as the pasta boils on.

Luigi: No, that wasn't it. Was it until the sun comes up? I'll try that.

Stop, stop, pasta pot.
I have my pasta, nice and hot.
There's enough to fill me up,
Until the sun comes up.

The pot continues to boil, and the pasta gets higher. Luigi watches. Pasta overflows, and Luigi jumps up and down in a panic. He looks at the pot again. Pasta is coming out the door. (Throw handfuls towards the door.) Luigi looks very scared. He runs out the door yelling. Benito walks out, shaking his head in disgust.

Luigi: Help! Help! I cannot stop the pasta. What shall I do?

The villagers look at the door in terror.

Giorgio: Luigi, you must do something! Stop the pasta pot! Why can't you stop it if you are so magico?

Francesca: What have you done? We've had enough pasta! Stop that pot from cooking right now! It is running all over our piazza. Stop it now, Luigi! We'll all be buried alive!

Soldier: We must save our town! Run and get pillows and blankets so we can stop the pasta. Subito!

The villagers run to their homes and get things to block the pasta. Luigi sits down and cries. The children run and hide. As the people start to return, they continue talking.

Salvatore: Luigi has ruined us! He is such a fool! What will happen to us?

Zingarella appears stage right and sees what is happening. She walks over to Luigi.

Zingarella: Luigi, will you never learn anything? I told you not to touch the pasta pot, but I see you did not listen. You are a silly fool, Luigi!

She wades through the pasta to the pot.

Zingarella: Stop, stop, pasta pot.
I have my pasta, nice and hot.
There's enough to fill me up,
Until the morning sun comes up.
Uno, due, tre.
Uno, due, tre.
Uno, due, tre.

The pot stops boiling, and the pasta ceases.

All Villagers: Grazie, Zingarella! Grazie! you have saved us!

Marco: Luigi, you almost ruined our village. You must leave, or you may make the same mistake again! Leave, Luigi, leave!

Villagers: Leave, Luigi! Leave our village and never return again!

 How to Do Plays with Children

Zingarella: Wait! There is a better way. Luigi meant no harm, and I think he has learned his lesson. Luigi, you wanted pasta, and pasta is what you shall have! Now you must eat all this pasta. I want to sleep in my bed tonight!

Zingarella gets a large fork and hands it to Luigi. He looks at the fork, at Zingarella, and then at the pasta. He dejectedly walks over to the pasta, bends over, puts the pasta on his fork, and begins eating. The villagers laugh and walk back to their homes. Soon the stage is empty except for Luigi who sits down, looks very sick, and eats the pasta. Curtain closes.

Curtain reopens. Each cast member is introduced and bows.

Italian Words

grazie (grah′zēā) - thank you

piazza (pē ahtz′zah) - square

addio (ah dē′ō) - goodbye

subito (sue′bē-tō) - hurry

uno (oo′nō) - one

due (doo′ā) - two

tre (trā) - three

basta (bahs′tah) - stop

ciao (chow) - goodbye

buon giorno (boo ōn gee ōr′nō) - good morning

benissimo (ben ē′si mō) - wonderful

How to Do Plays with Children

class:

presents the play

The Magic Pasta Pot

date:

time:

place:

Please join us!

The Magic Pasta Pot

Zingarella _____   Marco _____
Luigi _____   Pietro _____
Benito _____   Giuseppe _____
Maria _____   Giorgio _____
Michelangelo _____   Vincent _____
Anna _____   Leonarda _____
Rosanna _____   Anita _____
Geno _____   Soldier _____
Vito _____   Pasta Pot _____
Mario _____   Children _____
Giovanni _____   _____
Salvatore _____   _____
Katerina _____   _____
Domenic _____   _____
Francesca _____   _____

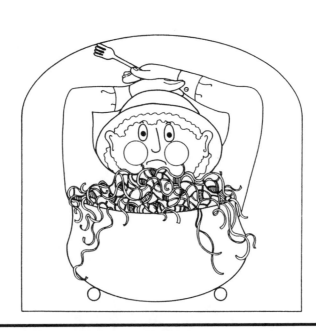

A Folktale Play
A Part for Everyone

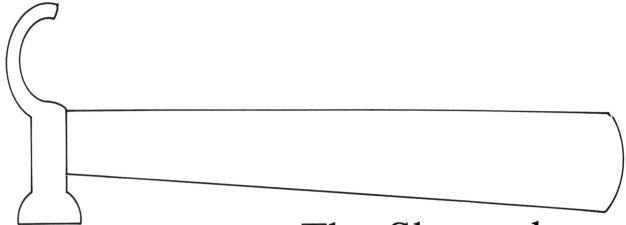

The Shoemaker and the Elves

A German Folktale
retold by Ginny Hall

Scenery 238

Characters and Costumes 240

Props 241

Script 242

Invitation 255

Play Program 256

Activities 257

Scenery

The **BACK WALL** can be made with large sheets of butcher paper. Paint the clock, pictures, and shelves before hanging the paper up. Attach the butcher paper to rolling chalkboards placed at each end. If you don't have rolling chalkboards, turn two long tables upright and stretch the paper between them. Attach with tape. Puppet theaters, refrigerator boxes, and flats may also serve as supports.

door

Create the **KITCHEN DOOR** by hanging fabric on a piece of doweling for a curtain effect.

The **WORKBENCH** is a long table with brown butcher, crepe, or shelf paper across the front to hide shoes and other things.

       How to Do Plays with Children

The **WINDOW WALL** can be created with cardboard from a refrigerator box, OR place a table where the wall is to be. Attach a long piece of doweling (standing up) to the right front table leg. Next, attach a piece of brown paper to the top of the doweling and stretch it to the back wall to form the top wall above the window.

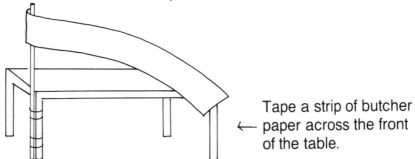

← Tape a strip of butcher paper across the front of the table.

CURTAINS can be cut out of colored paper or crepe paper.

THE EXTRA TOUCH — place potted flowers or plants outside the shop. If you have LOTS of energy and butcher paper, paint an outside background of shop fronts.

                                       How to Do Plays with Children

Characters and Costumes

HANS wears long pants or knickers, which can be created by tucking long pants into socks. He wears a cobbler's apron and glasses.

GRETCHEN wears a long dress or skirt and blouse. She usually has on an apron and a shawl. If you desire, the quality of her clothes can improve as the couple gets richer.

TOWN CRIER wears an old top hat and long jacket. Tails would be nice. His pants are very long and baggy; use a dad's pants. He carries a bell.

ELVES wear old shirts and pants with holes in them. Make them look as raggedy as possible. Their hair is always messed up. They are all barefoot.

SQUIRT is always the last one in and out.

STITCHY has a shoe sewn to his shirt. Tuck the shoe under the **shirt until he shows it to the audience.**
LIPPY, SMACKY, and POLLY each wear large glasses.

ZIPPO, DUSTY, and WIBBY each have swollen thumbs. This can be done by attaching a partially–blown-up pink balloon to their thumbs with tape or wrapping their thumbs with cloth.

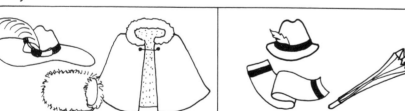

LISA, KATHY, MARIA, and ANN are rich women and should wear fancy long dresses or skirts and blouses. Elaborate hats could be borrowed or found at second–hand stores. Capes and muffs would be a nice touch.

WILHELM, FREDERICK, and JACOB are very rich and should wear suits or nice pants and a sportscoat. Hats would add a wonderful touch. The men can carry umbrellas or canes.

GIRL CHILDREN can dress like the women.

BOY CHILDREN can wear long pants or knickers, nice shirts, coats or jackets, and caps.

NARRATOR'S & SIGN CARRIER'S costumes are optional.

How to Do Plays with Children

Props

Check off

○ **PRESENTS FOR ELVES**
Wrap 13 boxes. Each box
contains one each of the
following: pair of socks
pair of pants
pair of shoes
shirt
jacket
hat

○ **SHOES**—Ten pairs of shoes.
Four pairs are needed to sell:
one pair of girl's brown shoes, pair
of boy's black boots, and two
pairs of girl's shoes in pretty
colors. Six pairs are made by the
elves as Hans and Gretchen
watch.

○ **BAGS or BOXES** to put the shoes
in when they are sold

○ **COAT RACK** for the shoemaker's
coat

○ **THREE HAMMERS** for the elves
and one for the shoemaker

○ **RAGS AND POLISH** for the elves
and shoemaker

○ **NAILS**

○ **LARGE SCISSORS**

○ **POTATOES**

○ **LARGE HEAD OF RED CABBAGE**

○ **SIGNS:** These can be painted
on long, wide pieces of butcher
paper. Roll up each end and
staple so they can be easily
held. You will need five signs:

> The Next Morning . . . . .
> Later That Day . . . . .
> Late That Night . . . . .
> Much, Much, Much Later . . .
> Late The Next Evening . . .

○ **BAG OF CABBAGE**—this can be
a pillow case stuffed with
newspaper.

○ **THREE LARGE NEEDLES**—
These can be made by twisting
two large pipecleaners together,
leaving a gap near the top to be
the eye of the needle.

○ **PLAY CASH REGISTER** that
rings is optional. A box will do.

○ **MONEY** — This can be made
by students. Make it large.

○ **SCISSORS** for the shoemaker

○ **RUG** for the store entrance

○ **BELL** for the town crier

○ **YARN** to thread through the
needles

○ **BROOM** to clean the shop

○ **PIECES OF LEATHER**

The Shoemaker and the Elves

A German Folktale
Script

Hans is in his shop cutting out leather for a pair of shoes.
Gretchen is standing next to him watching and holding a large head of cabbage.

Narrator: Many years ago in a clean, charming, small, quaint village in Germany there lived a kind, gentle, thoughtful, good-hearted, and very poor, by no fault of his own, of course, shoemaker named Hans (Hans bows) and his sweet, tidy, generous, kind and very poor wife named Gretchen (Gretchen bows). Times were bad, horrible, awful, and miserable; and the kind, gentle, thoughtful, good-hearted, and very poor, by no fault of his own, of course, shoemaker had not sold a pair of shoes for many days.

The town crier walks across the stage ringing his bell.

Town Crier: Six o'clock, and things are really awful!
Six o'clock, and things are really awful!

Gretchen: Hans, you have worked so hard, yet we have not a penny. We have eaten nothing but cabbage for weeks. We have no money to buy food to eat nor leather for new shoes. What are we to do? We will surely starve if someone does not buy this pair of shoes to-morrow.

Hans: Dear Gretchen, do not worry so. I know someone will want these shoes I am making. I will finish them tomorrow, and surely a kind person will come and buy them.

How to Do Plays with Children

Gretchen:	I hope you are right. You must be very hungry; I am. I am so tired of cabbage. I would love to taste bits of bacon and soft, fluffy potatoes tomorrow. Come. It is late, and you need your rest.	*Hans and Gretchen exit stage left. Sign carriers walk across the stage very slowly carrying sign "The Next Morning." While the sign is in front of the workbench, the leather is exchanged for a pair of pretty girl shoes so the audience will not see. The town crier walks across the stage ringing a bell and saying:*
Town Crier:	Nine o'clock in the morning, and life is full of surprises! Nine o'clock in the morning, and life is full of surprises!	*Hans and Gretchen enter the shop stage left. Gretchen is still carrying the head of cabbage. They stop just as they enter.*
Hans:	I must finish the shoes quickly. Soon people will be walking by, and surely someone will need a pair of shoes.	*They walk to the work bench, and both look very surprised. Hans picks up the shoes and inspects them.*
Hans:	Gretchen, the shoes are finished! Look at them. They are beautiful! It is a miracle!	
Gretchen:	They are the most wonderful shoes I have ever seen, Hans. Who could have done this?	
Hans:	I do not know, but I must put them in the window quickly. They are so splendid, I know they will be sold this morning.	
Gretchen:	Dear Hans, I do hope you are right, or it's boiled cabbage again today.	*Gretchen exits to the kitchen. Hans places the shoes in the window as Wilhelm, Maria, and Child 1 walk by. Maria looks at the shoes and becomes very excited.*

Maria: Oh, Wilhelm, these are the finest shoes I have ever seen! I must have them! I will pay twenty-five dollars for them. They are not sold are they?

Hans looks very surprised.

Hans: No, no they are not sold. I would be happy to sell them to you. Let me get them for you!

Maria: Oh, Wilhelm, I am so excited! I can wear these beautiful shoes to the ball at the castle tonight. They will look perfect with my new gown. Thank you! Thank you!

Hans takes the shoes from the window and puts them in a bag. Wilhelm hands Hans the money, and Wilhelm, Maria and Child 1 exit. Hans yells to Gretchen.

Hans: Gretchen! Gretchen! Come quickly!

Gretchen runs into the shop holding the cabbage.

Hans: Look, Gretchen, a man has just paid me twenty-five dollars for the shoes! Look! Look!

He holds the money to her face.

Gretchen: Hans, you have never sold a pair of shoes for that much money! We are rich! We can buy bacon and potatoes for supper tonight and enough leather for two pairs of shoes. I will go to the butcher shop and get the bacon, and you go buy more leather. How wonderful! I am so hungry. I can taste the crispy bacon right now.

Gretchen exits stage left happily. Hans puts on his coat and exits stage right, out the door. Sign carriers carry sign "Later That Day" across the stage. Hans comes on stage behind the sign and stands at the workbench. He is cutting out the leather. He whistles or hums a tune as he works. Gretchen enters stage left. She is still carrying cabbage.

Gretchen:	Hans, it is time for supper. Tonight we will have bacon and potatoes instead of boiled cabbage. I hope I never have to eat cabbage again. Have you finished cutting the leather for the shoes?	
Hans:	Yes, the leather is all cut. Tomorrow I will make the shoes. I had enough money to buy leather for three pairs of shoes. See how beautiful the leather is.	*Gretchen looks at the leather.*
Gretchen:	These shoes will be even better than the ones you sold today. Now come to dinner and taste the wonderful bacon and fluffy potatoes I have made!	*Hans and Gretchen exit through the kitchen door. Sign carriers carry sign "The Next Morning" across the stage. While sign is in front of the workbench, the leather is exchanged for three pairs of shoes - girl's brown shoes, boy's black boots, girl's pretty colored shoes. Town crier walks across the stage ringing the bell.*
Town Crier:	Nine o'clock in the morning and things are looking better! Nine o'clock in the morning and things are looking better!	*Hans enters the shop and sees three pairs of finished shoes on the work table. He looks very surprised and happy. He calls to Gretchen.*
Hans:	Gretchen, Gretchen, come quickly and see what has happened. Another miracle has taken place! All three pairs of shoes are finished! Gretchen, come quickly!	*Gretchen enters stage left, carrying the potatoes. She looks at the shoes, and jumps up and down excitedly.*
Gretchen:	Hans, this is wonderful! Who could have done this? They are such splendid shoes! Look at the workmanship. These will bring a good price. Quickly! Put them in the window so the people passing by will see them.	*Hans puts the shoes in the window and walks back to the bench.*

Gretchen: I must go clean the breakfast dishes and cook our lunch.

Ann: I must have the brown shoes in the window! You do wonderful work. They are the most beautiful shoes we have ever seen. I will pay you 30 dollars.

Gretchen exits as Ann, Kathy, Jacob and Child 2 & 3 walk to the window. They stop, look at the shoes and smile. They enter the store and stand by the window. Ann points to the shoes as she speaks.

Jacob: And I would like to buy the black boots. The craftsmanship is superb. I should be glad to pay fifty dollars for your fine work.

Hans: They are yours! I will wrap them for you. Wait just a moment.

He takes the shoes from the window and places them in a bag.

Kathy: Your shoes are the best I have ever seen. I will tell all of my friends that they must come to your shop to get their shoes.

Jacob and Ann: Thank you. Good day.

The customers leave the shop and Hans runs towards the kitchen door yelling.

Hans: Gretchen, Gretchen, we are rich! The lady and gentleman have paid us enough money to buy leather for six pairs of shoes!

Lisa, Frederick, and Child 4 enter the shop. Hans returns to help them.

Frederick: We would like to buy the shoes you have in your window, sir. They are wonderful and we must have them!

Lisa: We will pay you fifty dollars for the shoes. The are the most elegant shoes I have ever seen!

Hans: Of course, you must have them. They are wonderful shoes, and they will look magnificent on you. I will wrap them for you.

Hans gets the shoes and wraps them. Frederick hands him the money, and the customers exit the shop talking excitedly.

Lisa: They are lovely shoes! Thank you, Frederick. Thank you for buying them for me.

Frederick: Yes, Lisa. They are lovely. You're welcome.

Child 4: I want some shoes too! Can we come back another day and buy some shoes for me? Please! Please!

Frederick: Yes, we will come back tomorrow and see if the shoemaker has some shoes for you. Now let's go home.

Hans yells to Gretchen.

Hans: Gretchen! Gretchen! We have sold the last pair of shoes for 50 dollars!

He exits stage left. The town crier walks across the stage ringing his bell.

Town Crier: Twelve o'clock noon and things are looking up! Twelve o'clock noon and things are looking up!

Narrator: And so it went on. Each day the kind, gentle, thoughtful, good-hearted and not-so-poor shoemaker would buy more leather and cut it out. The next morning beautiful shoes would be sitting on the workbench. The kind, gentle, thoughtful, good-hearted and no-longer-poor shoemaker and his sweet, clean, generous, kind and no-longer-poor wife became very prosperous and had enough money to buy good food, nice clothes, and beautiful leather for new shoes. They were very happy, and they never ate cabbage again!

Sign carriers carry sign "Much, Much, Much Later" across the stage. The town crier walks across stage ringing the bell.

Town Crier: Nine o'clock in the morning, and everything is wonderful! Nine o'clock in the morning, and everything is wonderful!

Hans and Gretchen enter stage left, talking.

Hans: Gretchen, we are so lucky to be able to afford such good food and fine clothes. Who do you think is making the shoes? We must find out and thank them for helping us.

Gretchen: You are right Hans. We would still be eating cabbage if it were not for some kindly person who makes the shoes during the night.

Hans: I know! Let's hide behind the door tonight and see who comes and makes the wonderful shoes. Tonight we shall discover the secret! Let us go rest, so we can stay awake tonight and watch.

They exit stage left. Sign carriers carry the sign "Late That Night" across the stage. The Town Crier walks across the stage ringing the bell.

Town Crier: Twelve o'clock midnight, and here they come! Twelve o'clock midnight and here they come!

Hans and Gretchen walk into the shop and hide behind the door. The elves will enter stage right after singing one chorus of the following song off stage to the music of "Jingle Bells." The elves stand in front of the work-bench when they enter.

Elves: We are elves, helpful elves,
We've come to save the day.
We're the elves who make shoes,
While we dance and play.
Stitch and nail, stitch and nail,
Soon we will be done.
There'll be shoes to fill the shop,
Shoes for everyone.

Elves: Happy feet, snappy feet,
Our shoes will make you dance.
Feet of every size and shape,
Will want to skip and prance.
Big, fat feet; small, thin feet;
Feet with lumps and bumps.
Our shoes make feet, happy feet.
They'll make them want to jump!

Second chorus is sung as the elves enter stage right.

All the elves jump up.

Cobbie: Okay, elves, we'd better get started.
This night will be a long one. Look
how much leather there is to sew and
stitch and polish. The shoemaker has
become a very wealthy man, which
means we have much more work to do.

Elves: Okay, we're ready! Let's go to work!

*The elves take their places behind the workbench. Squirt gets the
broom and begins sweeping in front of the workbench. The following
songs are sung to the tune, "Here We Go Round the Mulberry Bush."
Zippo, Dusty, and Wibby hammer and nail while they sing. As they finish
singing, they replace the leather pieces with three pairs of shoes hidden
on the shelf below bench.*

**Zippo, Dusty,
and Wibby:**   We're the elves who hammer the nails,
Hammer the nails,
Hammer the nails,
We're the elves who hammer the nails,
Our thumbs are proof of that.

*The three elves hold up
their thumbs which are
huge and red.*

**Lippy, Smacky,
and Polly:**   We're the elves who thread the needles,
Thread the needles,
Thread the needles,
We're the elves who thread the needles,
We think we're going blind.

*Lippy, Smacky and Polly
thread needles as they sing.*

Stitchy, Cobbie, and Trippy: We're the elves who stitch and sew,
Stitch and sew,
Stitch and sew,
We're the elves who stitch and sew,
We never make mistakes!

The shoes are passed on to Stitchy, Cobbie and Trippy who pretend to sew the shoes as they sing.

Sparkles, Skippy, and Shiney: We're the elves who polish the shoes,
Polish the shoes,
Polish the shoes,
We're the elves who polish the shoes,
And make them shine and sparkle.

Stitchy shows the shoe that is sewn to his shirt. The shoes are passed to Sparkles, Skippy, and Shiney, who shine the shoes as they sing.

Squirt: I'm the elf who cleans the mess,
Cleans the mess,
Cleans the mess,
I'm the elf who cleans the mess,
Sometimes life isn't fair!

Squirt sweeps very slowly as he sings.

Squirt sweeps under the bench as the others continue their work and pass the shoes to each other. He finds the cabbage and holds it up.

Squirt: Look! Look what I found!

Shiney: What a nice head of cabbage.
I wonder how it got under there?

Dusty: I love boiled cabbage! Can we
take it home and cook it for lunch?

Smacky: I'll cook it. I love boiled cabbage too!

The elves clean up and put things away.

Squirt: Well, it looks like we're finished. This
is getting to be lots of work. I hope the
shoemaker doesn't get too much richer.

Cobbie: Okay, let's call it a night. Come on fellows,
the sun's almost up.

The elves exit stage right and sing, whistle, dance, and play as they walk off the stage. When they are gone Hans and Gretchen come out from behind the door where they have been hiding. They walk to the bench and look at the finished shoes.

Hans: These are such lovely shoes! Who would think thirteen little elves could do such fine work?

Gretchen: Hans, they have worked so hard to help us. We must do something for them. What can we do?

Hans: Did you see how tattered their clothes were? They didn't even have shoes to wear. Let's make clothes and shoes to keep them warm.

Gretchen: That's a wonderful idea, Hans! You are such a clever fellow! I can sew shirts and jackets for them. I will make them warm hats to wear. And you can make them each a pair of shoes. Let's get started right now, so we can surprise them tomorrow night.

Hans and Gretchen exit stage left. Sign Carriers carry the sign "Late That Evening" across the stage. Hans and Gretchen enter carrying packages wrapped in bright paper and a sack full of cabbages. They lay the things on the workbench.

Gretchen: Oh Hans, I hope they like the clothes we have made. They have been so kind and generous to us.

Hans: They will love the clothes and shoes. The clothes are lovely and will keep them warm on cold winter nights. Come, let us hide, for they will be here soon.

Hans and Gretchen hide behind the door again. After a few moments the singing elves can be heard. The elves sing as they enter the shop. The Town Crier walks across the stage ringing the bell.

Town Crier:	Twelve o'clock midnight. Time for the big surprise! Twelve o'clock midnight. Time for the big surprise!	*The elves enter after singing two lines off stage. The tune is to "Jingle Bells."*
Elves:	Here we come, here we come, Dancing all the way. We're the elves who make the shoes, While we dance and play. Stitch and nail, stitch and nail, Soon we will be done. They'll be shoes to fill the shop, Shoes for everyone!	*The elves can sing or whistle the song again if more time is needed to get on stage. They stand in front of the workbench.*
Cobbie:	Okay elves, let's go to work!	
Squirt:	I sure am getting tired of cleaning up all the time. I think it's someone else's turn to clean!	*Squirt sits down in the middle of the stage and pouts. The other elves go the workbench. Stitchy sees the packages on the workbench.*
Stitchy:	Look! What are these? Where is the leather for the shoes?	
Zippo:	These are sure pretty packages! Do you think these are for us?	
Smacky:	Who would leave us presents?	
Sparkles:	I'm pretty cute, maybe they are all for me!	
Dusty:	I'm cute too! Some of them must be for me!	
Skippy:	Well, let's open them and see what's inside.	*The elves tear open the packages and hold up the clothes. They laugh and dance around the room, putting on the clothes.*
Trippy:	These are the nicest clothes I have ever seen. Don't I look handsome! Look at me!	

How to Do Plays with Children

Polly: My shirt fits perfectly and this coat is so warm and nice!

Wibby: Look at me! Look how wonderful I look in my new shoes. They are as good as the shoes we make.

Lippy: Socks! Our feet will be toasty and warm. No more cold feet!

Polly: Look! This bag is full of cabbage. We can have boiled cabbage for a week.

All the elves cheer at this news. The elves show off their clothes to each other and prance around.

Cobbie: Shhh! We will wake the shoemaker and his wife. They must have made these clothes for us. Now that we look so fine, why should we make shoes any longer? Let's go home and have a party to celebrate our new clothes and no more work, for a while anyway.

The elves dance out the door as they sing to the tune of "Here We Go Round the Mulberry Bush."

Elves: We're the elves that look so fine,
Look so fine,
Look so fine,
We're the elves that look so fine,
No more shoes will we make!

The elves repeat the song until they are off stage right. When they are out of sight, the shoemaker and his wife come out from behind the door, smiling.

Hans: Did you see how happy they were, Hans? They loved the new clothes and shoes we made.

Gretchen: I am so glad they liked the presents we gave them. They have been so kind to us. Now we are very rich, and we will never have to eat boiled cabbage again!

253

Hans: Yes, the elves have made our lives wonderful. Come, Gretchen, let's get some rest. It has been a long day.

Hans and Gretchen exit stage left through the kitchen door.

Narrator: And so, as you might expect, the shoemaker and his wife lived happily ever after. The elves went back to the forest. A few days later they heard about a jolly old man who made toys and decided to go help. But then that's another story.

CURTAIN

Curtain!

 How to Do Plays with Children

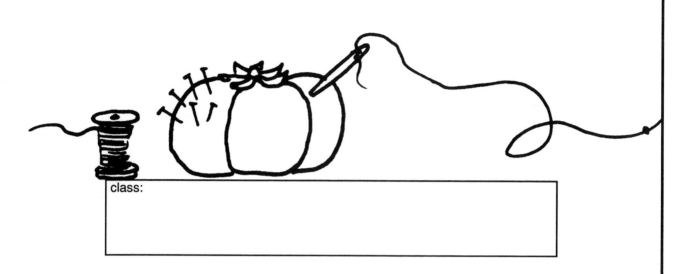

class:

presents the play

The Shoemaker
and the Elves

date:

time:

place:

Please join us!

255

Note: Program for play. Fill in the cast of characters.

The Shoemaker and the Elves

Cast

Narrator_____

Hans_____

Gretchen_____

Town Crier_____

Maria_____

Wilhelm_____

Child 1_____

Ann_____

Kathy_____

Jacob_____

Child 2_____

Child 3_____

Lisa_____

Frederick_____

Child 4_____

Sign Carriers_____

_____

_____

Elves

Cobbie_____

Zippo_____

Dusty_____

Wibby_____

Lippy_____

Smacky_____

Polly_____

Stitchy_____

Trippy_____

Sparkles_____

Skippy_____

Shiney_____

Squirt_____

The Shoemaker and the Elves
Sequencing

1. Get a piece of paper.
2. Read all the sentences below.
3. Write the sentences in the order in which they happened in the play.
4. Use your BEST handwriting.

○ Hans and Gretchen wrapped the presents.

○ Jacob bought a pair of black boots.

○ The elves decided to help make toys.

○ Hans and Gretchen watched the elves make the shoes.

○ Hans bought leather for three pairs of shoes.

○ Wilhelm paid twenty-five dollars for Maria's shoes.

○ Hans and Gretchen found one pair of finished shoes on the workbench.

○ Hans made shoes for the elves.

The Shoemaker & the Elves

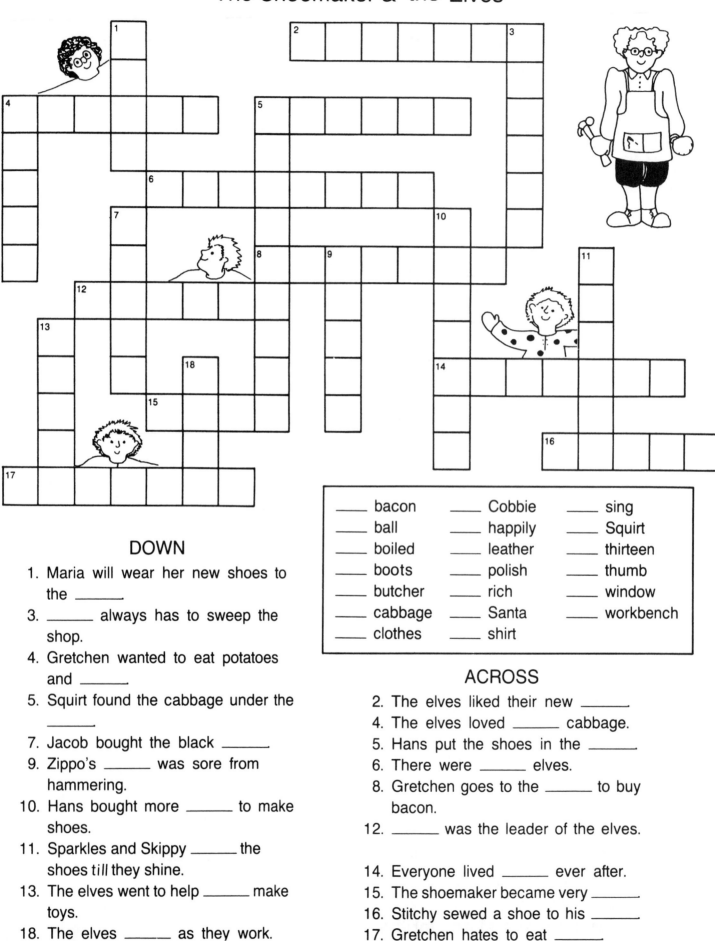

DOWN

1. Maria will wear her new shoes to the _____.
3. _____ always has to sweep the shop.
4. Gretchen wanted to eat potatoes and _____.
5. Squirt found the cabbage under the _____.
7. Jacob bought the black _____.
9. Zippo's _____ was sore from hammering.
10. Hans bought more _____ to make shoes.
11. Sparkles and Skippy _____ the shoes till they shine.
13. The elves went to help _____ make toys.
18. The elves _____ as they work.

_____ bacon	_____ Cobbie	_____ sing
_____ ball	_____ happily	_____ Squirt
_____ boiled	_____ leather	_____ thirteen
_____ boots	_____ polish	_____ thumb
_____ butcher	_____ rich	_____ window
_____ cabbage	_____ Santa	_____ workbench
_____ clothes	_____ shirt	

ACROSS

2. The elves liked their new _____.
4. The elves loved _____ cabbage.
5. Hans put the shoes in the _____.
6. There were _____ elves.
8. Gretchen goes to the _____ to buy bacon.
12. _____ was the leader of the elves.
14. Everyone lived _____ ever after.
15. The shoemaker became very _____.
16. Stitchy sewed a shoe to his _____.
17. Gretchen hates to eat _____.

How to Do Plays with Children

Part 5

Reader's Theater

Not all performances need to be formal plays where parts are memorized, sets are built, and costumes are made. Reader's Theater with its emphasis on reading aloud becomes an activity in which almost everyone can participate. Reader's Theater is also perfect for limited space and time. All you need are a few copies of the script and an area to use for staging. Stools, music, and lighting can be added, but even this is not necessary for a successful performance.

Choose materials suitable for the interests and reading levels of your students. This can be a play, a long poem, a series of short poems, etc. Think about the number of children you want to take part in the performance and the length of time you have for the performance.

Have students think about the character before they read aloud. Is the character old or young? brave or cowardly? gentle or mean? lazy, shy, happy, sad...? Practice reading the parts in appropriate voices. (If you have unsure readers, read the material aloud to them until they are comfortable with it.)

Don't be critical. This is supposed to be a joyful experience. Be gentle if you need to make suggestions on how to improve intonation, pronunciation or projection.

Let everyone in class be a part of the practice sessions by having those not reading practice their "audience" skills.

Provide enough practice time for students to become familiar with their lines so they can read with clarity and confidence.

Staging should be simple. Arrange children on the stage in a way that they can all be seen and heard clearly. Have some sit on chairs or stools. Have others stand or sit on the floor.

Provide a way for them to keep their pages together during the performance. It can be distracting to have pages flying out of hands. Staple the pages together in a cover, put them in lightweight binders, place them in folders on music stands, whatever works best for the age of your students.

Reader's Theater Scripts in Part 5

Cave Pet **261**

Do you Know About Whales? ··· **265**

The Gigantic Rutabaga (A Folktale of Russia) **269**

The Right Way to Ride a Donkey (A Folktale of Nigeria) **275**

The Three Brothers and the Singing Toad (A Folktale of Mexico) **282**

Cave Pet
Script
by Leslie Tryon

Characters
Reader
Child
Wolf

Reader: The little cave child inside the cave and the wolf pup outside the cave in the cold and the wind, study each other and wonder what it would be like to know one another. Since no child can resist a puppy and no puppy can resist a child, they decide to be pals. The child speaks first and then the wolf. The speaking partners go back and forth between the two characters.

Child: I'm lonely. I guess I'll just sit by the fire.

Wolf: I think it must be dangerous in there; I see a fire.

Child: Besides, it's really cold outside.

Wolf: It looks nice and warm in that cave and it's cold out here.

Reader: Finishing up a piece of meat, the child tosses the bone aside.

Child: I'm full.

Wolf: I'm hungry. I wonder if he would share that bone with me.

Child: I wish I could clean this grease off my hands.

Wolf: I could show him how to lick his hands clean.

Child: I'm sleepy. Mom and Dad are off on a hunt and I have to sleep alone.

Wolf: My pack has all gone off on a hunt. I don't have anyone to sleep with. I'm cold.

Reader: Looking at the wolf pup and thinking out loud, the child said,

Child: I wonder if he's lonely too.

Wolf: I think he must be lonely too. He doesn't have anyone around.

Child: Maybe he would come in here if I offered him this bone.

Wolf: He looks young like me. I don't think I'm afraid of him.

Reader: Cave child offers the bone to the wolf.

Child: Come on boy, you don't have to be afraid. We can keep each other company.

Reader: The wolf pup enters the cave very carefully, looking side to side, and behind himself. He keeps an eye on the fire.

Wolf: He's offering me that bone. It's warm in here - how nice.

Reader: The cave boy carefully strokes the wolf pup.

Child: This is nice. I've never been this close to an animal before.

Wolf: This is nice. I've never been this close to a human before. I've never let one touch me.

Child: In the morning we could go out and play. I could show him how to fetch.

Wolf: We could go out and play in the morning. I could show him how I can catch.

Child: I trust you. I'm going to go to sleep now.

Wolf: I think I trust you. I'll just curl up next to you and we'll both stay warm.

     How to Do Plays with Children

Wild Dog Word Search

```
A R C T I C F O X W O L F D
R F Z W O L F D J P U P W I
A G R A Y F O X O A X U O N
C P E I N G P Z W G C P L G
C U D W C X R U D O P K F O
O P F O O A Q A P O L U A X
O R O L Y P N V Y R G F P L
N E X F O U Z W U W T Z W B
D D W G T P J K I D O G O U
O W O F E N N E C L Z L L S
G O L P U P W O L F D R F H
R L F A D H O L E B V D X D
Z F X M A N E D W O L F O O
B A T E A R E D F O X W Z G
```

AFRICAN WILD DOG
ARCTIC FOX
BAT-EARED FOX
BUSH DOG
COYOTE
DHOLE
DINGO
FENNEC
GRAY FOX
GRAY WOLF
JACKAL
MANED WOLF
RACCOON DOG
RED FOX
RED WOLF

How many times can you find WOLF? _____

   How to Do Plays with Children

Do You Know about Whales?

Script

by Leslie Tryon

Characters
Chorus
Blue Whale
Fin Whale
Sperm Whale
Gray Whale
Killer Whale

How to Do Plays with Children

Chorus: The big yellow school bus,
Full of curious kids like us,

Drove right out to sea to see
Just how big a whale can be.

A giant of a whale swam right up to us and said...

Blue Whale: I'm the biggest whale. I'm the giant blue.
The earth's biggest creature. It's absolutely true.

From my fluke to my nose, a whale of a whale.
The length of three busses, placed nose to tail.

Chorus: WOW!
The big yellow school bus,
Full of curious kids like us,

Drove right out to sea to see
Just how big a whale can be.

Another big whale came speeding up to us and said...

Fin Whale: I'm the Fin. I'm fast 'cause I'm thin.
Two and a half busses long from end to end.

I have a bony moustache in place of teeth.
Only in the top jaw, there's nothing underneath.

Chorus: Bigger than two school busses. WOW!

The big yellow school bus,
Full of curious kids like us,

Drove right out to sea to see,
Just how big a whale can be.

HEY! This one really LOOKS like a whale.

Sperm Whale: I'm the square-nosed Sperm whale.
Two busses long, from my nose to my tail.

I live in the tropics where there's lots to eat.
But the giant squid is my favorite treat.

Chorus: Giant squid - Yuck!

The big yellow school bus,
Full of curious kids like us,

Drove right out to sea to see
Just how big a whale can be.

LOOK! Here comes another one.

Gray Whale: I'm one school bus long. I'm the gray,
I'm bumpy all over, from barnacles they say.

I love to breach, to jump out of the sea
And you may see the whale lice, all over me.

Chorus: Whale lice - that's nice.

The big yellow school bus,
Full of curious kids like us,

Drove right out to sea to see
Just how big a whale can be.

Hey! Here comes a two-toned whale.

Killer Whale: I'm called the killer whale you know.
I'm dark on the top and light below.

I'm one of the very best hunters in the sea.
Your school bus is just a bit bigger than me.

A Sea Mammal Word Search

```
C O M M O N D O L P H I N F B W W D O
W A U P W H A L E Y B W K L R H H A T
H H L P Y G M Y A W O H I Y Y A A L R
U W A I W E B A T H W A L S D L L L I
M H E L F H E L P A H L L P E E E S S
P A W O E O A N U L E E E O S I F P S
B L H T E A R L E E A T R D W R I O O
A E A S P I N N E R D O L P H I N R S
C W L W A L L A I W H A L E A G W P D
K H E U L A W R W A W M W Z L H H O O
S W I M G A H W H T G H I H E T A I L
W H A L E A W H A L E R A N A P L S P
S P E R M W H A L E S E A L K L E E H
A L E B O T T L E N O S E Y E E E M I
Y A N G T Z E R I V E R D O L P H I N
```

BELUGA	MINKE
BLUE	NARWHAL
BOWHEAD	PILOT
BOTTLENOSE	PYGMY
BRYDE'S WHALE	RIGHT
CALIFORNIA GRAY	RISSO'S DOLPHIN
COMMON DOLPHIN	SEI
DALL'S PORPOISE	SPERM WHALE
FIN WHALE	SPINNER DOLPHIN
HUMPBACK	YANGTZE RIVER DOLPHIN
KILLER	

How many times can you find WHALE in this word search? _____

 How to Do Plays with Children

The Gigantic Rutabaga

A Folktale of Russia
Script

Retold by Betsy Franco

Reader #1	Grandfather	Sharik the Dog
Reader #2	Grandmother	Moorka the Cat
Reader #3	Granddaughter	Mwishka the Field Mouse

Reader #1:   Grandfather Stefan spent most of his time in the vegetable garden. Above the ground grew rows and rows of cabbage, peas, and cucumbers. Under the ground grew rows and rows of carrots, onions, potatoes, beets, and Grandfather's favorite vegetable — rutabaga. One particular rutabaga started, just like others, as a tiny seed. It grew a little each day until one morning, Grandfather couldn't help but notice that it had become gigantic. Grandfather cried,

Grandfather: This gigantic rutabaga will feed us for the whole winter! Won't Grandmother be surprised!

Reader #2:   Grandfather grasped the leafy top of the rutabaga and pulled.

All readers: He pulled very hard
and gave a shout,
But the rutabaga
would not come out.
That plant was stuck,
There was no doubt.

Reader #2:   He called to Grandmother...

Grandfather: Baba, I need your help with this gigantic rutabaga.

Reader #2:   Grandmother dropped her basket of peeled kartoshka, ran over, and grabbed Grandfather from behind. Grandmother pulled on Grandfather, and Grandfather pulled on the rutabaga.

All readers: They pulled very hard
and gave a shout,
But the rutabaga
would not come out.
That plant was stuck,
There was no doubt.

Reader #2: With her sides heaving, Grandmother
yelled to her granddaughter for help,

Grandmother: Anna, we need your help with this gigantic rutabaga.

Reader #3: Granddaughter set down the rag doll
she was making, skipped over and
grabbed Grandmother around the
waist. Granddaughter pulled on
Grandmother, Grandmother pulled
on Grandfather, and Grandfather
pulled on the rutabaga.

All readers: They pulled very hard
and gave a shout,
But the rutabaga
would not come out.
That plant was stuck,
There was no doubt.

Reader #3: Catching her breath, Granddaughter
called to the dog...

Granddaughter: Hey there Sharik, we need your
help with this gigantic rutabaga.

Reader #1: The dog stopped chasing his tail,
trotted over, and grabbed
Granddaughter's sash. The dog
pulled on Granddaughter, Granddaughter
pulled on Grandmother, Grandmother pulled
on Grandfather, and Grandfather pulled on the
rutabaga.

All readers: They pulled very hard
and gave a shout,
But the rutabaga
would not come out.
That plant was stuck,
There was no doubt.

Reader #1:   The dog licked his sore paw and
yelled for the cat to help..

Dog: You there, Moorka, we need your
help with this gigantic rutabaga.

Reader #2:   The mangy old cat stopped stalking
birds, slunk over, and grabbed the
dog around the middle. The cat
pulled on the dog, the dog pulled on
Granddaughter, Granddaughter
pulled on Grandmother, Grandmother
pulled on Grandfather, and
Grandfather pulled on the rutabaga.

All readers: They pulled very hard
and gave a shout,
But the rutabaga
would not come out.
That plant was stuck,
There was no doubt.

Reader #2:   The cat sat down, her tongue hanging
out, and yelled for the field
mouse to help...

Cat: Mwishka, we need your help with
this gigantic rutabaga.

Reader #3:   The tiny field mouse stopped
searching for seeds, scurried over,
and held onto the cat with her tiny
paws. The mouse pulled on the
cat, the cat pulled on the dog, the
dog pulled on Granddaughter,
Granddaughter pulled on Grandmother,
Grandmother pulled on Grandfather, and
Grandfather pulled on the rutabaga.

All readers: They pulled very hard
and gave a shout,
AND THE RUTABAGA
FINALLY CAME OUT!!!

Russian Words in the story:

kartoshka (kahr-tohsh´-kah) -- potatoes
Sharik (Shah-reek´) -- typical name for a Russian dog
Moorka (Moor´-kah) -- typical name for a Russian cat
mwishka (mwihsh´-kah) -- mouse

The Gigantic Rutabaga

How to Do Plays with Children

The Right Way to Ride a Donkey

A Folktale of Nigeria

Script

Retold by Betsy Franco

Reader #1	Tunde (father)	Villager #3
Reader #2	Villager #1	
Reader #3	Villager #2	

Reader #1: Under a roof of palm leaves in a small village in the bush country of Nigeria lived a man named Tunde. Tunde was very restless and very eager to travel. On the day of the New Yam Festival he announced,

Father (Tunde): My son and I must go on a long journey to learn about the world. We have so much to learn that cannot be taught in our small village.

Reader #2: The very next morning, Tunde and his young son packed plenty to drink and a supply of yams for making foo-foo. They both mounted their chocolate brown donkey and set off on their journey. After traveling for days through lush rainforest, they came to a large village. There they found themselves in the middle of a marketplace with endless rows of goods for sale -- brightly colored fabrics, slabs of goat meat, calabashes, sparkling jewelry, and much, much more. Perched on their donkey, Tunde and his son were very excited about all the commotion.

Father (Tunde): I wonder what we'll learn today.

All readers: The young son heard his father say. But soon the donkey drew a crowd and people stared and laughed out loud.

 How to Do Plays with Children

Reader #2: Everywhere, the people were jabbering and pointing at Tunde and his son.

Villager #1: Look there, a man and his son, both riding a donkey.

Villager #2: Has the old man no heart?

Villager #3: That poor tired donkey is being mistreated!

Reader #2: Upon hearing this, Tunde grew more excited.

Father (Tunde): My son, we are learning things already. If we hadn't left our village, we never would have known what we were doing wrong. I'll walk and you ride the donkey alone.

Reader #3: Tunde and his son traveled in this way for many days through forests and plains until they came to a second large village.

Father (Tunde): I wonder what we'll learn today.

All readers: The young son heard his father say. But soon the donkey drew a crowd and people stared and laughed out loud.

Reader #3: Again the people pointed and talked loudly about Tunde and his son.

Villager #1: "I've never seen such a sight!"

Villager #2:   The old man walks while his
son rides the donkey!

Villager #3:   Don't children show respect
for their parents anymore?

Reader #3:   Tunde listened to the talk and
thought and thought. He was
getting very confused. He said...

Father (Tunde):   My son, we are learning so much
about the world! Now we know
more than before. I must ride the
donkey and you must walk.

Reader #1:   Tunde mounted the donkey and his
young son walked beside him. After
many, many long days, they came
to a third village in the middle of a
sandy plain. Many of the men
wore flowing white robes. It was a
sight to behold!

Father (Tunde):   I wonder what we'll learn today.

All readers: The young son heard his father
say. But soon the donkey drew a
crowd and people stared and
laughed out loud.

Reader #1:   Again the people spoke loudly
among themselves.

Villager #1:   Can you believe what you see, my
friend?

Villager #2:   A grown man makes his young son
walk while he rides in comfort!

Villager #3: Every father should know to take care of his child before himself.

Reader #1: As Tunde listened, he grew very, very confused. He thought and thought and finally he said,

Father (Tunde): My son, we learn something new each day. We should not be riding the donkey at all.

Reader #2: Tunde got off the donkey and walked beside his son until they came to a fourth village. The people walking by looked very elegant. Some rode camels.

Father (Tunde): I wonder what we'll learn today.

All readers: The young son heard his father say. But soon the donkey drew a crowd and people stared and laughed out loud.

Reader #2: Again the people gathered and pointed.

Villager #1: Who are this man and his son that they walk alongside a donkey?

Villager #2: They are tired and yet they do not ride.

Villager #3: Surely the sun has taken away their senses!

Reader #2:   Tunde listened, and this time wrinkles formed between his eyebrows as he thought and thought for a long time. Finally he said,

Father (Tunde):   My son, it is definitely time to go home. We have learned so much on our journey. What some people say is the right thing to do, other people say is the wrong thing to do. Hop back on the donkey. We will both ride the donkey as we did at the start of our journey!

Reader #3:   Tunde and his son both mounted the donkey and set out for their small village in the south of Nigeria. The father leaned over to his son and said,

Father (Tunde):   If you listen, you can learn a lot in the world. But, in the end, you must always use your common sense and do what you think is right.

Nigerian Words in the Story:

foo-foo (FOO-foo) -- a dough-like snack made from yam or grain

yam (yam) -- staple food of West Africa; similar to a sweet potato

calabash (ca-la-BASH) -- a container made from a gourd that has been hollowed out

---

The Right Way to Ride a Donkey

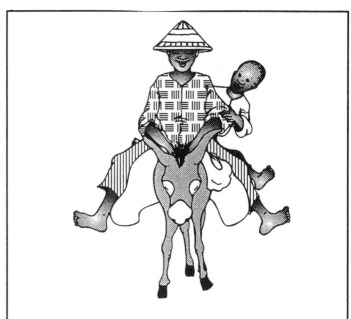

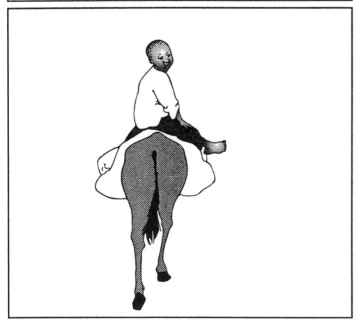

281   How to Do Plays with Children

The Three Brothers and the Singing Toad

A Folktale of Mexico

Script

Retold by Betsy Franco

Reader #1	Father	Toad
Reader #2	Oldest Son	Bird (girl)
Reader #3	Second Son	
Reader #4	Youngest Son	

Reader #1: There was an old farmer with three sons who took great pride in his large and well-kept corn field. He was terribly unhappy one day when he realized that a large, mysterious animal was stealing his corn. The farmer called his three sons to his side,

Father: A thieving animal is destroying my corn. I will give my cornfield and everything I own to whichever of you can bring the animal back...dead or alive.

Reader #1: The oldest son set out first.

Oldest Son: All I need to complete this deed, father, is a good horse, a gun, and some atole. I will be back soon enough.

Reader #1: When he had ridden nearly half the distance to the cornfield, he came to a deep cenote where he could rest and water his horse. Beside the cenote sat a small toad singing happily. The toad said,

Toad: I'm just a small, brown, singing toad, but listen carefully, To catch the tricky cornfield thief, you'll need a gift from me.

Reader #1: The oldest son, feeling tired and hot, snapped back,

Oldest Son: Why should I listen to a small toad?

Reader #1:   Then he picked up the brown toad, flung it into the deep cenote and continued on to the cornfield. Once there he sat through the hot afternoon and on into the dark and lonely night, until his eyelids were drooping with tiredness. But the thieving animal never appeared.

Reader #2:   When the oldest son returned home, he entered the house with his head down. His father, who could see that he had failed, said,

Father: Since you have not completed the task, you cannot claim my cornfield and all that I own. Now it's your brother's turn.

Reader #2:   The second son jumped up, ready to go.

Second Son: All I need is a gun and some atole, and I should be back by dusk.

Reader #2:   When the second son reached the cenote, the toad was still there, singing his happy song. The toad said,

Toad: I'm just a small, brown, singing toad,
but listen carefully,
to catch the tricky cornfield thief,
you'll need a gift from me.

Second Son: Keep quiet, simple toad, I'm trying to rest. I do not need the help of a toad, and I never will.

Reader #2: At that, he picked up the toad by one leg and tossed it head first into the deep cenote. After a siesta to refresh himself, the second son hiked over to the cornfield. To his surprise, he spotted a large bird with beautiful white wings amidst the corn. As the bird took flight, the second son raised his gun and shot at it. Two large, milk-white tail feathers floated down from the sky, but the bird escaped. The second son collected the feathers and trudged home. On the way he made a plan.

Second Son: I have found and killed the thieving animal. I present you with its tail feathers.

Reader #2: But his father and two brothers were not fooled.

Father: You have only the feathers of the bird. You have not finished the task. Now it's your brother's turn.

Youngest Son: All I need is a gun and some atole, please, father. I will bring back the whole bird.

Reader #3: When the youngest son reached the cenote, the toad was singing his song cheerily. He said,

Toad: I'm just a small, brown, singing toad,
but listen carefully,
to catch the tricky cornfield thief,
you'll need a gift from me.

Reader #3: The youngest son was pleased to see the toad and he replied,

Youngest Son: Oh thank you, small toad, for offering your help. Here, take some of my food. If you help me find the thief, I will keep you with me forever.

Reader #3:   The toad was delighted, he said...

Toad: At the bottom of the cenote is a magic stone. It will grant you any wish.

Youngest Son: I would only wish for a kind and lovely wife and a way to catch the thieving animal that is stealing my father's corn.

Toad: Your wish will be granted this very day, not only that, but you will have a spacious home to live in with your new bride. Come with me to the cornfield.

Reader #3:   As they approached the cornfield a large graceful bird appeared from behind a tree. The youngest son took aim, but the toad jumped at his leg to stop him. Just then, the bird spoke,

Bird (girl):   Please do not shoot me. I am not really a bird, but a girl! An evil witch did this to me when I refused to marry her son. If you shoot me, you will be killing your own bride. You must believe me.

Reader #3:   The youngest son was most surprised. But then he realized that his wish was coming true!

Youngest Son: Come with me, white bird, and I will take you home to my father and my brothers. With the toad's help and the promise of the magic stone, you will surely become a woman again, and you will be my bride.

          How to Do Plays with Children

Reader #4: The farmer and his other sons were shocked to see the youngest son entering the doorway of the house with a large, white bird and a small brown toad.

Youngest Son: I have brought you the thieving animal you asked for, father. But it is really a woman who was cruelly bewitched. With the toad's help and the stone's promise, she will be changed before your eyes.

Reader #4: The toad sang his song heartily. The room became silent except for the toad's singing. Before their eyes, the white bird changed into a lovely young woman. Out the window, all could see a spacious home where none had been before.

Father: You have found the thief, my son, as well as a lovely bride. You shall receive my cornfield and all that I own in return.

Reader #4: The youngest son married the young woman, and they lived in the spacious home with the farmer, who was very happy in his old age. The two older brothers, who were jealous and disgusted, ran off and were never seen again. The small brown toad sat every day on the patio of the house and sang his cheerful song.

Spanish Words in the Story:

cenote (seh-noh´-teh) -- a deep natural limestone well
atole (ah-toh´-leh) -- drink made from corn
siesta (see-ehs´-tah) -- afternoon nap